P9-DUI-557

ACCLAIM FOR FAYE LEVY

"Faye Levy has studied and taught cooking in France, Israel, and the United States. She ranks among the most imaginative and careful of all cookbook authors, so her recipes are inspirational and accurate."

—*Boston Herald*

"As an instructor and inspiration in the kitchen, Faye Levy is without peer. . . . Levy gives us clear, concise, exhaustive instructions. Without talking down to us, she hovers over, guides, encourages. Goof-ups are practically impossible. And the results are terrific."

—Maureen Clancy, *San Diego Union*

"Levy is one of our brightest new cookbook authors. As meticulous and painstaking as she is creative, Levy, always the teacher, gives impeccable instructions."

—*Cleveland Plain Dealer*

"Levy is one of the most knowledgeable and reliable food writers in the country."

—Judith Hill, food editor, *First for Women*

"Levy is one of America's top culinary columnists and authors."

—*Elle* magazine

"I'm partial to any cookbook by Faye Levy. Her recipes always work and the information she imparts is always easily understood by every level of cook."

—Muriel Stevens, *Las Vegas Sun*

OTHER BOOKS BY FAYE LEVY

Faye Levy's International Vegetable Cookbook

Faye Levy's International Chicken Cookbook

Faye Levy's International Jewish Cookbook

Sensational Pasta

Sensational Chocolate

Fresh from France: Dessert Sensations

Fresh from France: Dinner Inspirations

Fresh from France: Vegetable Creations

Classic Cooking Techniques

La Cuisine du Poisson (in French, with Fernand Chambrette)

Faye Levy's Favorite Recipes (in Hebrew)

French Cooking Without Meat (in Hebrew)

French Desserts (in Hebrew)

French Cakes, Pastries and Cookies (in Hebrew)

The La Varenne Tour Book

30 LOW-FAT MEALS IN 30 MINUTES

Faye Levy

WARNER BOOKS

A Time Warner Company

If you purchase this book without a cover
you should be aware that this book may have been stolen property
and reported as "unsold and destroyed" to the publisher.
In such case neither the author nor the publisher
has received any payment for this "stripped book."

Copyright © 1995 by Faye Levy
All rights reserved.

Warner Books, Inc., 1271 Avenue of the Americas, New York, NY 10020

Visit our Web site at http://warnerbooks.com

W A Time Warner Company

Printed in the United States of America
First Printing: March 1995
10 9 8 7 6 5 4

Library of Congress Cataloging-in-Publication Data

Levy, Faye.
    30 low-fat meals in 30 minutes / Faye Levy.
      p. cm.
    Includes index.
    ISBN 0-446-67059-6
    1. Quick and easy cookery. 2. Menus. 3. Low-fat diet—Recipes.
I. Title. II. Title: Thirty low-fat meals in 30 minutes.
TX833.5.L48   1995
641.5'638—dc20   94-30636
                                              CIP

Book design by Giorgetta Bell McRee

ATTENTION: SCHOOLS AND CORPORATIONS
WARNER books are available at quantity
discounts with bulk purchase for educational,
business, or sales promotional use. For
information, please write to: SPECIAL SALES
DEPARTMENT, WARNER BOOKS, 1271 AVENUE
OF THE AMERICAS, NEW YORK, N.Y. 10020

*Dedicated to the memory of
Gregory Usher and Robert Noah,
Americans in Paris,
quintessential culinary professionals,
dear friends*

CONTENTS

Introduction

Cooking at home is the key to a healthful diet. In our own kitchens we control what goes into our meals. When we eat out, however, we must trust strangers who may not really care about our nutritional needs. So why doesn't everyone eat in more? Many of us are busy and have little time to spend in the kitchen.

In this book my goal is to solve this dilemma by providing a month's worth of easy, light, and lively menus. The menus and the many tips on cutting time and eliminating fat from your cooking are a good starting point. Once you are comfortable with these menus, you may be inspired to create many more low-fat, thirty-minute meals for you, your family, and your friends.

My guidelines are to follow the advice of most nutritionists: use as little saturated fat as possible and limit the calories that come from fat to 30 percent or less. In this book, the menus have an average of 25 percent of their calories from fat; some go as low as 10 percent, but none is over 30 percent. Following these low-fat menus will make a dramatic difference in most people's diets.

People often ask me why I am not overweight. They figure that, as a culinary professional, I must cook and taste a lot. I tell them that in my family, too, cooking with little fat is important. However, instead of going on diets, we simply cook nutritious food most of the time.

The first cookbooks I wrote featured many recipes rich with butter and cream. Over the years I have reduced the fat more and more. In this book, I take my quest for healthful food one step further by keeping within the 30 percent fat guidelines.

In *30 Low-fat Meals in 30 Minutes*, I have challenged myself to create healthful menus, with an emphasis on speed. However, because of my classical French culinary training, I refuse to compromise taste. The result of these seemingly conflicting goals is a book of delicious yet quick low-fat meals.

Even in trimming the fat from our food, moderation is the secret to success. If you reduce the oils too drastically and the food is no longer tasty, chances are you will soon give up the pursuit of healthful eating. But if your meals are pleasing instead of punishing, it is easy to keep to a nutrition-conscious eating plan.

Although some of the recipes in this book are suitable for entertaining, the emphasis is on menus for everyday cooking. Most menus are designed for family meals and for quick, casual suppers with friends.

The menus follow today's flexible dining habits. Most include three recipes but do not necessarily follow the traditional pattern of first course, main course, and dessert. Sometimes there is a main course with two accompaniments, or a salad, a main course, and a side dish.

I use fresh ingredients as much as possible, although in the interest of speed I do buy a few ready-to-eat foods. I don't buy prepared salad dressings, for example, since it's so easy to make quick and tasty dressings at home.

For timing the menus, I assume you already have the ingredients and pots at hand. If you hunt for your oregano for ten minutes and find you must run to the store, there's no way the menu will be ready in half an hour!

Some of the menus may take more than thirty minutes the first time you prepare them. After you are familiar with a menu and know which pans and utensils you like to use for each dish, you will go faster.

Nobody wants to spend much time cleaning, especially when there's little time to cook. In developing these recipes, I have used as few pots and pans as possible to save on cleanup time.

I hope you will find these speedy, simple low-fat meals great tasting. Remember, it's best not to say no to fat, but to say "just a little." I wish you happy and healthful cooking and eating!

30 Low-Fat Meals in 30 Minutes

CHAPTER 1

STRATEGIES FOR QUICK, LOW-FAT COOKING

There are many ways to serve freshly made home-cooked meals in minutes instead of ordering pizza or serving TV dinners. The key to fast and easy low-fat meals is an overall strategy that includes efficient shopping, menu planning, and cooking. By choosing fresh, lean ingredients that cook rapidly, by using streamlined cooking techniques, and by keeping a selection of the right items in your pantry, you can gain time in the kitchen while cutting fat from your diet.

SHOPPING

Economizing on time and minimizing fat begin before you enter the kitchen. Efficient shopping is an important step in achieving these goals. Be sure your pantry contains the makings of quick, low-fat meals for those days when you don't have a chance to buy fresh ingredients. (See list of pantry ingredients, page 4.)

Choose Fast-Cooking Meats and Fish that Are Also Lean

Boneless chicken breasts, turkey breast slices, ground chicken and turkey, fish fillets, scallops, and shrimp are prime examples of desirable meats. In some markets you can find ground turkey breast, the leanest ground meat of all.

Many markets now offer different types of lean ground beef; at my local market you can buy it with 15 or 7 percent fat. At many markets the type lowest in fat is called "extra-lean." Naturally, choosing the leanest version makes a big difference in the amount of fat in your menus.

If you're cooking steak, use the leaner Select grade of beef rather than Choice or Prime, and choose the lower-fat cuts such as top sirloin, top round, or tenderloin. Flank steak is fine too, but it requires marinating before broiling or grilling. Lamb and veal loin chops and pork tenderloin are other fairly lean meats with brief cooking times.

Whichever cut you choose, always trim the visible fat. Even chicken breasts often have small blobs of fat that should be cut off before the meat is cooked.

For quick cooking when you don't have much time to shop, keep frozen fish and seafood on hand. Individually frozen shrimp and scallops thaw swiftly and can even be cooked from the frozen state.

Use Ready-to-Eat Meats and Fish as Ingredients

Fish departments of well-stocked supermarkets usually carry cooked shelled shrimp, cooked crabmeat, cooked lobster tails, smoked fish, and barbecued fish. You can also find smoked fish in the deli section, as well as smoked and roasted meats such as roast turkey and lean roast beef. These are flavorful additions to cooked pasta, rice, and salads, turning them into satisfying main dishes. If used judiciously, they don't add much fat.

Use Plenty of Vegetables and Fruit

We all know that eating a generous amount of vegetables and fruit is a key to good health. There is a wealth of choices for incorporating them effortlessly into your menus.

Check out the produce section of your supermarket. New, ready-to-eat fresh ingredients seem to be coming in every month. You can buy beautiful, delicate, mixed baby lettuces; robust romaine lettuce leaves in bite-size pieces; and hearty escarole mixed with endive and radicchio. With so many varieties of cleaned, ready-to-eat greens on display, there is no excuse for serving meals without salads.

And there's more than just lettuce. Another health-promoting vegetable that comes prepared is cabbage. You can buy shredded red and green cabbage at most markets, sometimes sold as "coleslaw mix." Or try "broccoli slaw" made of shredded broccoli stems, carrots, and red cabbage; it's delicious with just a tiny bit of oil and vinegar.

Busy cooks no longer have to stem and wash fresh spinach, as rinsed spinach leaves are readily available in packages. Fresh broccoli florets, cauliflower florets, sugar snap peas, asparagus spears, banana squash sticks, and carrot slices are sold in microwave-safe trays. You can prepare these ready-to-cook vegetables by a variety of methods, not just steamed in the microwave. For a main-course vegetable, make use of soaked black-eyed peas, which are available in bags and cook in only fifteen minutes.

Alongside the carrot sticks, celery sticks, and cleaned radishes, you are likely to find jicama sticks, cantaloupe balls, fresh diced watermelon, and pineapple cubes. Prepared, ready-to-eat raw vegetables and fruits are useful to have on hand as snacks, as quick appetizers, or even to munch on while you're preparing dinner!

At home we don't have apprentices or helpers as restaurant chefs do. So let the store do your *mise en place,* or preparation. Buy your broccoli already trimmed, your mushrooms sliced, and your spinach washed.

In planning menus, choose from the following categories:

1. Vegetables that cook rapidly and are simple to prepare: Broccoli, cauliflower, zucchini, crookneck squash, green beans, sugar snap peas, snow peas.
2. Ready-cut and cleaned fresh vegetables: Shredded green and red cabbage, peeled baby carrots, shredded or sliced carrots or carrot sticks, shredded celery root, broccoli slaw, cleaned spinach, sliced mushrooms, rinsed lettuce mixtures, broccoli and cauliflower florets, celery sticks, jicama sticks, cleaned radishes.
3. Frozen vegetables: Peas, lima beans, black-eyed peas, corn, mixed vegetables such as a Chinese medley that includes water chestnuts.
4. Canned vegetables: See list of pantry ingredients, page 4.
5. Fresh seasonal fruit: Both cut and whole, for desserts and snacks.
6. Frozen fruit: Especially berries, for making quick sauces, sorbets, and other desserts.

Have a Pantry Well Stocked with Quick-Cooking, Low-Fat Ingredients

Most traditional cuisines rely on a few key bottled, canned, or dried ingredients as flavorings. These staples allow people to whip up a meal in minutes, and include main-course foods as well as seasonings to enhance recipes. Keep these valuable pantry items on hand for fast, light cooking, so that weekday shopping is easier.

1. Staples from the base of the USDA food pyramid: Many of these staples can be the basis for a meal—pasta in a variety of shapes; couscous, white rice, instant brown rice, bulgur wheat. In your freezer, keep fresh pasta, which is now available in light and low-cholesterol varieties, as well as lighter versions of stuffed pastas.
2. Canned and bottled vegetables: Bottled roasted peppers, canned diced chiles, peeled tomatoes, diced tomatoes, water chestnuts, marinated artichokes, and marinated mushrooms add interest to rice and pasta dishes, salads, meat and vegetable medleys, and many other dishes. Canned corn and beans of many types, such as chickpeas, black beans, and white beans, are convenient foods for practically instant main courses. Choose beans canned in water and salt, rather than in sauces that contain fat.
3. Canned fish: Tuna and salmon are handy for a quick lunch, with pasta, rice, or good bread and a green salad.
4. Bold seasonings: Choose seasonings that instantly add flavor with no effort and no need for long simmering. Some examples are sun-dried tomatoes (both dry-pack and oil-pack), dried mushrooms, dried herbs, spices, wine, extra-virgin olive oil, walnut oil, sesame oil, herb vinegar, mustard, capers, a few bottled Chinese sauces, canned chicken and vegetable broth, and canned tomato sauce.
5. Frozen desserts: Don't forget the freezer as a source of low-fat desserts. Keep frozen berries for making quick sauces and toppings, and good-quality sorbets and low-fat frozen yogurts for snacks and desserts.

COOKING TECHNIQUES

To get a good meal on the table in short order, it helps to be organized. Try a new approach to cooking. Devise a plan of action to make the best use of your time. Have several simple dishes going at the same time. Instead of preparing all the ingredients before starting to cook, dice one ingredient while another is cooking.

Cook by various techniques, not necessarily those you have always used. Focus on the rapid methods and use them with less fat.

Broil and Grill

Grilling, barbecuing, and broiling may be the most popular cooking techniques in America. With their delectable, slightly charred crust, meat, poultry, and fish cooked by these methods are most appealing. And the food is not only delicious but also fast-cooking and low in fat. "Meaty" vegetables such as eggplant, mushrooms, and peppers also taste great when grilled.

For rapid cooking, choose broiling or grilling over baking or roasting. Broiling is more practical for speedy cooking than charcoal barbecuing; after all, coals take about half an hour to heat up, while the broiler is hot almost instantly. It's also much easier to check the food for doneness when it is in the broiler than on the barbecue. When grilling, use a gas barbecue or stovetop grill to save time, rather than waiting for charcoal to heat. Use a minimal amount of oil to brush on the food to keep it moist; with red meats, you can omit the oil.

Like grilling, broiling is a dry-heat cooking method. The food is set on a rack, so the heat circulates underneath and the food doesn't steam. But to minimize cleanup time, you can put the food on a double piece of foil.

Simple seasoning is best for broiled or grilled foods, especially in the case of fish. A little salt and freshly ground pepper, a dash of cayenne, and a sprinkling of thyme, oregano, or rosemary are all you need, plus a little fresh lemon juice and olive oil to rub on the fish so it won't dry out as it cooks.

Broiled fish is a superb choice for low-fat cooking in minutes and is easier to prepare than grilled fish. Many broiler racks have nonstick surfaces, but fish often adheres stubbornly to grill racks. And of course, in the broiler there is no problem of bits of fish falling into the coals as the fish is turned over.

The Canadian method of cooking fish, allowing ten minutes per inch of thickness, works well in the broiler. On the grill, the fish cooks slightly faster. To check if the fish is done, insert the point of a thin sharp knife into the center of the fish and look inside: the flesh should look opaque; in other words, it should have the color of cooked rather than raw fish.

Chicken or turkey should always be cooked until well done. Check with a knife; the meat should no longer be pink. Try not to overcook the meat on the grill or in the broiler, however, or it will be dry. To minimize dryness, use a stovetop grill rather than a broiler for cooking boneless, skinless chicken and turkey.

Grilling and broiling are excellent techniques for quickly cooking steaks and chops. Remember to serve fairly small portions to keep the meal low in fat.

Low-Fat Sauté or Stir-Fry

Choose sautéing or wok cooking as a speedy way to cook boneless chicken, turkey, lean beef, and vegetables such as onions, mushrooms, bell peppers, and zucchini. Even when you use just a little oil, it imparts a lovely flavor to the food.

To use these techniques in low-fat cooking, follow these guidelines:

1. Use just enough vegetable or olive oil or oil spray to barely cover the base of the pan with a thin layer. Oil spreads as it heats, so you should add even less than enough oil to cover if the pan is cold. If you have poured too much oil in the pan, wipe off the excess with a paper towel.
2. Use a heavy pan so the food won't burn, especially if very little oil is added.
3. Sauté the food with the lid on instead of uncovered. This way you take advantage of the steam to help keep the food moist. This technique is perfect for poultry and vegetables.

FAYE LEVY

Quick-Braise

Choose brief braising as a leaner alternative to classic sautéing or stir-frying. Traditional braising is designed for long, slow cooking of tough meats but quick braising is ideal for tender meat and poultry.

Begin by sautéing the food in a little oil, then add canned broth or other liquid to finish cooking. This is a wonderful technique for steaks (as in Beef Tenderloin with Mushrooms and Red Wine, page 15), turkey breasts, boneless chicken breasts (as in Speedy Sweet-and-Sour Chicken, page 41), and vegetables (as in Easy Eggplant Stew, page 99).

Poach in Sauce or Soup

Cook fish, shellfish, chicken breasts, and tender vegetables in sauces or soups instead of in water and then preparing a separate sauce. This not only cuts down on the number of pots you use but also makes serving simple. Some examples of this cooking method are Cioppino (page 73), in which scallops and shrimp cook in a tomato-wine sauce or Quick Chicken-Noodle Soup with Broccoli and Garlic (page 36).

Boil

If you need a large pot of boiling water to cook pasta, rice, or vegetables, put the pot of water on the burner before you do anything else and cover the pot to make the water boil faster. Cooking in boiling water is very fast, but bringing a large potful of water to a boil takes a long time.

Boiling is a favorite European way to cook green vegetables rapidly so they retain their vivid green color and crisp-tender texture. The technique is especially suitable for cooking broccoli, green beans, sugar snap peas, snow peas, and zucchini. The vegetables are added to a saucepan containing enough boiling salted water to generously cover them, and they are boiled uncovered over high heat. Root vegetables such as carrots, potatoes, and turnips are added to cold water, brought to a boil, and simmered in a covered pot until tender.

Drain the vegetables well in a strainer before serving them, and season them lightly with salt, pepper, and if you like, a squeeze of fresh lemon juice and a few drops of olive oil.

Steam

An alternative to boiling that is almost as fast for cooking vegetables, steaming keeps in more of a vegetable's nutrients. Spinach, zucchini, snow peas, and potatoes benefit enormously from this technique. Steaming is also an ideal way to cook scallops and shrimp.

Use Your Microwave

The microwave oven is a terrific time-saver for cooking vegetables. For example, winter squash can fit in a thirty-minute menu if you microwave them. I also like to use the microwave to cook potatoes, sweet potatoes, artichokes, and corn on the cob.

Fish, too, cooks well in the microwave. Many recipes for broiled fish can instead be cooked in the microwave, cutting the cooking time from about ten minutes to three minutes for one pound of fish.

Remember the value of the microwave for reheating leftovers, from cooked vegetables to meat or fish in sauce, to cooked grains.

Chop and Shred Vegetables in Your Food Processor

Use your food processor often to shred cabbage, carrots, and other vegetables, and also to chop onions. Small quantities of garlic or parsley are easier to chop in a mini food processor.

Keep your food processor handy, if possible, so you won't spend time and effort lifting it out of a cabinet.

Use Canned Broths and Other Prepared Ingredients

Shorten the preparation time of long-cooking dishes such as soups by using canned chicken or vegetable broth. With the broth as a tasty base, you can have a satisfying soup by adding fast-cooking ingredients such as fine noodles and frozen or diced fresh vegetables, and briefly simmering them in the soup.

High-quality flavored pasta can be a basis for a main course that is a snap to prepare; you just cook the pasta with a cut vegetable and drizzle the mixture with olive oil.

Learn to Prepare Several Recipes at the Same Time

While the main course is simmering, you can throw together the salad ingredients. Be sure you have several timers to use as reminders.

Don't worry if one dish is ready before the others. Simply turn off the heat and reheat the food later, if necessary. With experience, you'll gain a sense of which foods can wait.

Use Good-Quality Pans

Heavy pans, especially those with a quality nonstick surface, help you gain speed and cut fat. They make it possible to use less oil without letting the food burn, and to sauté food rapidly over relatively high heat.

MENU PLANNING

Rethink your menus. A meal doesn't have to have an appetizer, main course, and dessert. For a quick, low-fat dinner, prepare a main course and round it out with sliced vegetables, excellent bread, and seasonal fruit. Even plain pasta, rice, or other grain topped with a well-seasoned cooked vegetable can make a pleasant meal.

Prepare Salad as a First Course

If you serve salad first, when you're most hungry, you and your family will eat more of the healthful greens and less of the high-calorie foods that usually follow. In most markets, colorful mixed baby lettuces, romaine lettuce, iceberg lettuce, and other mixtures of greens are available in packages. They enable us to add nutrients and appeal to our menus instantly.

To make a savory green salad, all you do is open the bag, pour the amount of greens you want into your salad bowl, and add dressing. If you lose no time in getting your bowl out of the cupboard and your bag of greens out of the refrigerator, this can take under a minute!

For dressing, I'm not wild about the commercial concoctions. Making your own vinaigrette takes practically as little time as using prepared dressing and gives you much better control over flavor and nutritional value.

Instead of opening a bottle of Italian dressing, for example, you open one bottle of oil and one of vinegar, and add a small splash of each to your greens. Use about half or one-third as much vinegar as oil, then sprinkle the salad with salt and pepper. Toss the greens well and the salad is ready.

Of course, oil of superb quality gives the finest flavor. Extra-virgin olive oil is the most popular, while walnut and hazelnut oils make pleasant variations. Vegetable oils such as safflower or canola oil also make tasty dressing, especially if paired with aromatic vinegars such as tarragon, raspberry, balsamic, or sherry vinegar. Or substitute fresh lemon juice for the vinegar; cut a lemon in half and squeeze the juice through a small strainer right into the salad. You can also accent the dressing with flavorings such as mustard, chopped shallots, garlic, and fresh or dried herbs.

Occasionally you might like to serve green salad after the main course in the French tradition, but you can easily make it a refreshing first course. All you need do is top the greens with an appetizing ingredient—cooked baby shrimp, a few pieces of smoked fish, sliced mushrooms, strips of roasted peppers, citrus fruit sections, or toasted nuts.

Here's a salad dressing rule I was taught at a cooking school in Paris: don't drench the greens with dressing. The French refer to dressing for green salad as *assaisonnement*, or seasoning, rather than sauce. The dressing should season the leaves and very lightly moisten them, but there should never be a pool of dressing at the bottom of the bowl. This advice is even more important today, when so many of us are trying to reduce the fat in our diets. In this case, good health and good taste go hand in hand.

Choose Some Dishes that Can Wait

If all the dishes in your menu are sautés, it can be difficult to have them ready to serve at the same time. Most grain dishes can be cooked ahead and left covered until you wish to serve them. Food in sauce or soup can simply be covered and will stay warm; if necessary, they can be briefly reheated on low heat.

Cook Enough for Twice

Whenever you have more time to cook—on weekends, for example—prepare larger quantities of food so you have leftovers. When roasting meat or poultry, choose a larger roast. If you're cooking white or brown rice, cook double the amount; the extra rice reheats beautifully in the microwave. Make double batches of tomato sauce, spaghetti sauce, and chicken soup and freeze the extra portions. They provide the quick makings of another meal.

Even vegetables, although they cook in a short time, come in handy if you have some already cooked. With green vegetables, rinse them with cold water once they are cooked to keep their color green. To use, warm them by dunking them for a minute in boiling water, or heat them in a covered dish in the microwave.

Prepare One-Dish Meals

One-dish meals based on pasta, rice, or beans cooked briefly with meats or vegetables will save time in both cooking and serving. Often, you can cook pasta or rice with a vegetable at the same time, then simply drain them and add seasonings and perhaps a bit of cooked turkey or other meats.

Whole-meal soups such as Minestrone in Minutes (page 118) also make satisfying meals. Just add crusty bread, perhaps a salad, and fruit for dessert.

Buy the Best Bread You Can Find

Excellent bread is a great contribution to a meal. The finest breads taste wonderful even without butter. If you don't have time to stop at a bakery, you can find good bread at well-stocked supermarkets. Vary your breads to keep your meals interesting.

Snack on Produce

What if you've prepared a low-fat menu and you're still hungry, or you get "the munchies" between meals? Reach for fruit. Enjoy a cool, crisp apple or a sweet, juicy peach. If the fruit you buy isn't satisfying you, look for better produce at other markets or at fruit and vegetable shops. Find out which market in your area has the finest produce. Talking to your local store manager might improve the quality there, too.

Choose Low-Fat Beverages

Fresh juices of excellent quality are available in most markets. They make a delicious, fat-free snack.

When serving coffee, take a tip from the French and the Italians. Serve it black or use low-fat milk instead of cream; even nonfat milk makes excellent foam for cappuccino.

CHAPTER 2

MEAT AND POULTRY MENUS

Filet Mignon Feast for Two

- *Beef tenderloin with mushrooms and red wine* -
- *Sugar snap peas with shallots* -
- *Fresh baguette or other crusty French bread* -
- *Crepes with creamy berry filling* -

AMOUNT OF CALORIES FROM FAT: 30%

Dinner with a French touch is a treat that does not have to be high in fat. Filet mignon, or beef tenderloin, is the most tender cut of beef and is also fairly lean. To turn the meal into a celebration, why not enjoy a glass of wine, such as a Bordeaux or Cabernet Sauvignon, with the main course? For dessert, treat yourself to crepes with a luscious strawberry and "cream" filling made with nonfat sour cream. If you have a few more minutes, prepare Strawberry Sauce (page 74) and pour it around the crepes.

13

ALTERNATIVES:

⇨ Substitute snow peas, thin asparagus, or green beans for sugar snap peas.

⇨ Instead of a cooked vegetable, serve a Salad of Baby Lettuces (page 27).

GAME PLAN:

Step 1. Boil water for cooking peas.
Step 2. Trim peas; slice shallots; cook peas and drain.
Step 3. Prepare meat and sauce.
Step 4. Prepare dessert.

TIPS:

♥ Use Select instead of Choice or Prime beef. It has less marbling and thus is leaner.

☺ Ready-to-eat crepes, often sold in the produce section, make it possible to have glamorous desserts in minutes.

BEEF TENDERLOIN WITH MUSHROOMS AND RED WINE

2 small beef tenderloin steaks (about 10 ounces total)
1 tablespoon vegetable oil
Salt and freshly ground pepper
1 (6-ounce) package sliced fresh mushrooms (about 3 cups)
¼ cup dry red wine
¼ cup canned beef broth
½ teaspoon dried thyme

Trim all visible fat from beef. Cut beef in 1-inch dice.

Heat oil in a heavy nonstick skillet or sauté pan. Add beef, sprinkle with salt and pepper, and sauté, shaking pan often, over high heat about 2 minutes, then over medium-high heat 1 minute or until brown. Leave cubes medium-rare inside; cut one to check. Remove meat.

Add mushrooms to pan and sauté over medium heat about 2 minutes or until lightly browned. Add wine and bring to boil. Add broth, thyme, salt, and pepper. Boil 2 minutes or until most of the liquid evaporates. Return beef to sauce and heat over low heat. Taste and adjust seasoning. Serve hot.

Makes 2 servings.

SUGAR SNAP PEAS
WITH SHALLOTS

½ pound sugar snap peas, rinsed and ends removed
2½ teaspoons vegetable oil
4 medium shallots, peeled and sliced
Salt and freshly ground pepper

Add peas to a heavy medium saucepan of boiling salted water and boil uncovered over high heat 2 minutes or until crisp-tender. Drain in a colander, rinse with cold water, and drain well.

Heat oil in the saucepan over medium-low heat. Add shallots and sauté about 3 minutes or until tender. Add peas, sprinkle with salt and pepper, and sauté over medium heat until heated through.

Makes 2 servings.

CREPES WITH CREAMY BERRY FILLING

1 teaspoon sugar
½ cup sliced strawberries
½ cup nonfat sour cream
½ teaspoon vanilla extract
2 packaged crepes, room temperature
2 whole strawberries, for garnish

Sprinkle the sugar over sliced berries and mix. Mix sour cream and vanilla. Add to strawberries and mix well.

Reserve 2 teaspoons filling. Spoon half of remaining filling onto edge of each crepe and roll up in cigar shape. On each plate next to crepe, spoon 1 teaspoon filling and top with a whole strawberry.

Makes 2 servings.

Southern-Style Steak Menu

- *Barbecued sirloin steaks with garlic* •
- *Easy corn maquechou* •
- *Coleslaw with mustard dressing* •
- *White or sourdough dinner rolls* •
- *Watermelon, sliced peaches, or cherries* •

AMOUNT OF CALORIES FROM FAT: 23%

For a Fourth of July cookout, try sirloin steak with a tangy Texas marinade of red wine vinegar, garlic, and a little oil. Colorful Corn Maquechou with onion, bell peppers, and tomatoes is not burning hot, in spite of its Cajun roots; black pepper and cayenne are added with restraint. This dish is not only quick and easy, it's also convenient—you can make it ahead and keep it for two days in the refrigerator. With the fruit after the dinner, you might like to serve vanilla frozen yogurt.

ALTERNATIVES:

⇨ For a flavorful coleslaw variation, use packaged fresh broccoli slaw made of shredded broccoli mixed with a bit of carrot and red cabbage, instead of grated cabbage.

⇨ In summer, you might prefer a Saint Tropez Tomato Salad (page 68) instead of or in addition to coleslaw. In spring, celebrate the Southern love for sweet onions by preparing a green salad with Vidalia onions: follow the recipe for Avocado, Red Onion, and Romaine Salad (page 108), using Vidalia or other sweet onions and omitting the avocado.

⇨ Instead of Corn Maquechou, vary the menu by preparing corn on the cob either in the microwave or on the grill. In winter, you can substitute microwaved yams or sweet potatoes for the corn.

Game Plan:

Step 1. Marinate steak.
Step 2. Prepare corn.
Step 3. Make coleslaw.
Step 4. Grill steak.

Tips:

♥ Before cooking steaks, be sure to trim fat well, or buy steaks from a market that does it for you.

☉ The fastest way to make coleslaw is to use packaged shredded cabbage, or coleslaw mix, made of shredded green cabbage with a small amount of carrot and red cabbage. Otherwise, shred cabbage in a food processor.

BARBECUED SIRLOIN STEAKS WITH GARLIC

1¼ pounds top sirloin steak, about 1 inch thick
1 large garlic clove
1 tablespoon vegetable oil
2½ teaspoons red wine vinegar
Coarsely ground black pepper
Salt

Trim all visible fat from steak. In a mini food processor, chop garlic, add oil and vinegar, and blend well. Rub mixture over steak. Let marinate about 10 minutes. Meanwhile, heat a gas or charcoal grill or stovetop grill.

Sprinkle the steak with coarsely ground pepper. Grill about 4 or 5 minutes per side for medium-rare; cut to check. Sprinkle with salt and serve.

Makes 4 servings.

EASY CORN MAQUECHOU

1 tablespoon vegetable oil
1 medium onion, chopped
½ medium green bell pepper, diced
1 pound frozen corn kernels (3⅓ cups)
1 (14½-ounce) can diced tomatoes, drained
1 teaspoon sugar
Black pepper to taste
¼ teaspoon cayenne pepper, or to taste
Salt to taste

In a skillet, heat oil and stir in onion and green pepper. Cover and
sauté over medium heat 5 minutes, stirring occasionally. Add corn,
tomatoes, sugar, black pepper, and cayenne. Mix well. Heat until
sizzling. Cover and cook over medium-low heat, stirring often, 8 to
10 minutes or until corn is tender. Season to taste with salt and black
pepper; add more cayenne if needed. If desired, cook uncovered 1
to 2 minutes to evaporate excess liquid. Serve hot.

Makes 4 servings.

COLESLAW WITH MUSTARD DRESSING

1 tablespoon Dijon mustard
½ cup nonfat sour cream
½ teaspoon tarragon vinegar
2 teaspoons vegetable oil
1 (8-ounce) package coleslaw mix (shredded cabbage with
    carrots), or 4 cups shredded green cabbage
Salt and freshly ground pepper

In a small bowl, mix mustard with sour cream, vinegar, oil, and 2 teaspoons water until blended. Toss with coleslaw mix in a serving bowl. Season to taste with salt and pepper.

Makes 4 servings.

Mediterranean Veal Dinner

• *Braised veal chops with tomato-sage sauce* •
• *Orzo with saffron and zucchini* •
• *Salad of baby lettuces* •
• *Nectarines, plums, grapes, or pears* •

AMOUNT OF CALORIES FROM FAT: 30%

The robust flavors popular in Mediterranean cuisines are ideal for quick, light cooking. Lean, tender, fast-cooking veal loin chops gain wonderful taste from cooking in a tomato sauce accented with garlic, onion, and sage. Alongside it serve orzo, or rice-shaped pasta, which has a satisfying, almost creamy texture even when cooked with little or no oil. A fresh salad of baby lettuce sprinkled lightly with white wine vinegar and extra-virgin olive oil completes this elegant dinner. In summer, you might like to conclude the meal with an easy dessert of Nectarines in Red Wine (page 69).

ALTERNATIVES:

⊂⟩ Substitute bone-in chicken breasts for veal chops. Cook them for about 20 minutes.
⊂⟩ Serve Mediterranean Chopped Salad (page 78) instead of green salad.

GAME PLAN:

Step 1. Chop onion for veal and for orzo dishes in food processor; use half for each recipe.

Step 2. Cook veal and orzo simultaneously:
 a. Brown veal; meanwhile sauté onion for orzo.
 b. Sauté onion for veal.
 c. Add broth to orzo and cook.
 d. Cook veal in tomato sauce.
 e. Dice zucchini and add to orzo.

Step 3. Prepare salad.

TIPS:

♥ Use extra-virgin olive oil in salads—a little goes a long way.

☺ Buy rinsed, ready-to-eat baby lettuce in bags or in bulk.

BRAISED VEAL CHOPS WITH TOMATO-SAGE SAUCE

4 veal loin chops, about ¾ to 1 inch thick (about 8 ounces each)
Salt and freshly ground pepper
2 tablespoons olive oil
½ medium onion, minced
2 medium garlic cloves, chopped
1 (28-ounce) can diced tomatoes, drained
1 tablespoon chopped fresh sage, or 1 teaspoon dried, crumbled
1 tablespoon chopped fresh parsley (optional)

Trim all visible fat from chops. Pat dry. Sprinkle veal on both sides with salt and pepper. Heat oil in a large heavy skillet over medium-high heat. Add veal and brown it, in batches if necessary, about 2 minutes per side. Transfer to a plate.

Add onion to pan and sauté about 5 minutes over medium heat. Stir in garlic, then tomatoes and sauté 2 minutes. Add salt, pepper, and half the sage.

Return veal to skillet with any juices on plate and bring to a simmer. Cover and cook over low heat 4 or 5 minutes per side or until veal is tender and cooked to your taste; meat should be white or light pink. Add remaining sage to sauce. Taste, adjust seasoning, and serve sprinkled with parsley.

Makes 4 servings.

ORZO WITH SAFFRON AND ZUCCHINI

1 tablespoon olive oil
½ medium onion, chopped
1⅓ cups orzo or riso (rice-shaped pasta)
1 (14½-ounce) can chicken broth plus water to make 2⅔ cups
⅛ teaspoon saffron threads
2 medium zucchini, diced (about ⅓-inch dice)
Salt and freshly ground pepper

Heat oil in a medium saucepan. Add onion and sauté 3 minutes over medium heat. Add orzo and cook over low heat, stirring, 1 minute. Add broth mixture and saffron, stir, and bring to a boil. Cover and cook over low heat 8 minutes.

Scatter zucchini on top and sprinkle with salt and pepper. Cover and cook about 7 minutes or until orzo is just tender. Taste and adjust seasoning.

Makes 4 servings.

SALAD OF BABY LETTUCES

1 quart mixed baby lettuces
2 teaspoons extra-virgin olive oil
1 teaspoon white wine vinegar
Salt and freshly ground pepper

If greens are not already rinsed, rinse them and dry thoroughly. Transfer to a bowl. Add oil, vinegar, salt, and pepper to taste. Toss thoroughly and serve.

Makes 4 servings.

Springtime Lamb Dinner with Middle Eastern Flavors

- Grilled lamb chops with cumin •
- Easy bulgur wheat pilaf with mushrooms •
- Asparagus with roasted peppers •
- Strawberries, sliced kiwis, or pears •

AMOUNT OF CALORIES FROM FAT: 30%

I love lamb chops in the Middle Eastern style—cumin gives them such a lovely aroma. Although lamb chops are rich, when served with a fat-free accompaniment like bulgur wheat pilaf, they can still be part of a low-fat meal. Bulgur wheat is available in health food shops and in Italian, Greek, Armenian, Israeli, Iranian, and other Mediterranean and Middle Eastern grocery stores. If you would like to add a quick salad to this dinner, throw together a Salad of Baby Lettuces (page 27), using rinsed, ready-to-eat greens. Mediterranean Chopped Salad (page 78) or Cucumber Salad with Yogurt and Mint (page 143) also go well with this menu.

ALTERNATIVES:

⇨ Instead of bulgur wheat, prepare the side dish with couscous, and reduce the cooking time to 5 minutes; or substitute tabouli mix, which is bulgur wheat combined with spices.

⇨ If you wish to prepare the asparagus ahead or you have some left over, serve it cold as a salad and add a few thin half-slices of red onion separated in slivers. Or substitute broccoli for the asparagus.

GAME PLAN:

Step 1. Season lamb.
Step 2. Begin cooking bulgur wheat.
Step 3. Quarter mushrooms; add to bulgur.
Step 4. Heat water for asparagus; trim asparagus.
Step 5. Cook lamb.
Step 6. Cook asparagus.

TIPS:

♥ Traditional recipes for bulgur wheat call for sautéing it in oil, but it also gains a pleasing, nutty taste from being dry-roasted.

☉ Bottled roasted red peppers save a lot of time. They add color and superb flavor instantly to many dishes.

GRILLED LAMB CHOPS
WITH CUMIN

8 loin or rib lamb chops, about 1½ inches thick
2 teaspoons vegetable oil
Pinch of salt
1 tablespoon ground cumin
1 teaspoon turmeric
About ¼ teaspoon ground black pepper or cayenne

Trim all visible fat from chops. Brush both sides lightly with oil and sprinkle with salt. Mix cumin, turmeric, and pepper and sprinkle on both sides of lamb. Let stand while grill is heating. Heat a gas grill with rack about 4 to 6 inches above heat source; or have ready a stovetop ridged grill pan.

Grill lamb on heated grill until done to your taste; for medium-rare, allow about 5 to 7 minutes per side. Cut meat to check for doneness. Serve immediately.

Makes 4 servings.

EASY BULGUR WHEAT PILAF WITH MUSHROOMS

1⅓ cups medium bulgur wheat
2 large garlic cloves, minced
2 cups chicken broth, vegetable broth, or water
6 to 8 ounces fresh mushrooms, quartered
½ teaspoon dried thyme
¼ cup chopped fresh parsley (optional)
Salt and freshly ground pepper

In heavy medium saucepan, dry-roast the bulgur wheat with the garlic over medium heat, stirring, 2 minutes. Add broth and bring to boil. Reduce heat to low, cover, and cook 5 minutes. Add mushrooms, thyme, and ⅔ cup hot water. Cover and cook about 10 minutes or until water is absorbed and bulgur wheat is tender. Stir in parsley. Season to taste with salt and pepper.

Makes 4 servings.

ASPARAGUS WITH ROASTED PEPPERS

1½ pounds thin asparagus
Salt
1 cup strips of roasted or grilled red bell peppers (bottled or
   homemade, page 167)
2½ teaspoons extra-virgin olive oil
1½ teaspoons strained fresh lemon juice
Freshly ground pepper

Cut off about 1 inch from asparagus bases and discard. Rinse asparagus well. Cut each spear into 3 pieces.

Pour enough water to easily cover asparagus into a sauté pan, add salt, and bring to a boil. Add asparagus and boil about 2 minutes or until just tender when pierced with a sharp knife. Drain in a colander and transfer to a serving dish. Add peppers and mix gently.

In a small bowl, whisk oil with lemon juice, salt, and pepper. Pour dressing over vegetables and mix gently. Taste and adjust seasoning. Serve hot or at room temperature.

Makes 4 servings.

Chicken Soup for Supper

> • *Barbecued cod on iceberg lettuce* •
> • *Quick chicken-noodle soup with broccoli*
> *and garlic* •
> • *Rye bread with caraway seeds or fresh pita bread* •
> • *Pear and kiwi salad with dried cranberries* •
>
> —————————— AMOUNT OF CALORIES FROM FAT: 15% ——————————

Hot soup, especially chicken soup, makes a welcome winter main course. To prepare tasty, satisfying chicken soup without long simmering, briefly cook diced chicken, leeks, and carrots in prepared chicken broth. Before the soup, serve a basic green salad garnished with a bit of smoked or barbecued fish. The fish enhances the flavor of salads the way bacon does, but of course it is much lower in fat. For dessert, prepare the colorful winter fruit salad, and you'll see that it's as appealing as one made of summer fruits.

ALTERNATIVES:

⇨ If you have cooked chicken or turkey, cut it into bite-size pieces and heat it in the soup.

⇨ Omit the noodles and top each soup portion with about ½ cup of hot cooked white or brown rice.

Game Plan:

Step 1. Prepare soup.
Step 2. Cut vegetables for appetizer salad.
Step 3. Cut kiwis, prepare lime juice for fruit salad.
Step 4. Finish appetizer salad.
Step 5. Cut pears; finish fruit salad.

Tips:

♥ Cooking chicken breasts gently in soup is a good way to keep them moist.

☺ A fast way to make interesting fruit salad is to combine 2 fresh fruits and 1 dried fruit.

BARBECUED COD ON ICEBERG LETTUCE

4 cups iceberg salad mix
1 green onion, chopped
1 tablespoon extra-virgin olive oil
½ tablespoon wine vinegar
Salt and freshly ground pepper
2 medium plum tomatoes
3 ounces barbecued cod, in ¼-inch-thick strips (about ¾ cup)

In a salad bowl, toss salad mix and green onion with oil, vinegar, salt, and pepper. Cut tomatoes in eighths. Put tomatoes around edge of bowl. Place cod in center of salad and serve.

Makes 4 servings.

QUICK CHICKEN-NOODLE SOUP WITH BROCCOLI AND GARLIC

1 large leek, white and light green parts only
1 pound skinless, boneless chicken breasts
1 large carrot, peeled and thinly sliced
2 (14½-ounce) cans chicken broth
1⅓ cups fine egg noodles or other thin soup noodles
3 cups small broccoli florets
3 medium garlic cloves, minced
¼ teaspoon hot red pepper flakes
½ teaspoon dried thyme
Freshly ground black pepper
Salt (optional)

Quarter leek lengthwise, rinse well to remove sand between layers, and cut into thin slices. Trim visible fat from chicken and cut meat into 1-inch chunks. In a large saucepan, combine leek, chicken, carrot, chicken broth, and 2½ cups water. Bring to a simmer. Cover and cook over low heat 5 minutes.

Add noodles, broccoli, garlic, and pepper flakes and return to a simmer. Cover and cook over low heat about 6 minutes or until chicken and noodles are tender. Stir in thyme and black pepper to taste. Taste before adding salt; if broth was salty, it may not be needed.

Makes 4 servings.

PEAR AND KIWI SALAD WITH DRIED CRANBERRIES

1 tablespoon strained fresh lemon or lime juice
1 tablespoon sugar
2 kiwifruits
2 ripe medium pears
3 tablespoons dried cranberries, dried cherries, or raisins

Mix lemon juice and sugar in a small cup. Peel kiwis, halve, and slice each half. Transfer to a serving bowl. Core and slice pears; add to serving bowl. Add lemon juice mixture and toss. Add cranberries, toss, and serve.

Makes 4 servings.

Chinese Chicken Dinner

• *Shrimp salad with greens* •
• *Speedy sweet-and-sour chicken* •
• *Steamed rice* •
• *Stir-fry of peppers and green onion* •
• *Fuji apples or Asian pears* •

AMOUNT OF CALORIES FROM FAT: 18%

This is a Chinese menu without endless chopping, and with very little oil. Yet it still has that flair that makes Chinese cuisine so popular. For the main course, cook lean chicken breasts directly in a zesty sweet-and-sour sauce, which keeps the chicken moist as it cooks. The sauce is based on a recipe I learned from Chinese cooking teacher Mei Lee. It is a beautifully simple formula: equal amounts of ketchup, sugar, vinegar, and soy sauce—ingredients you most likely have in your pantry.

ALTERNATIVES:

⇨ Instead of shrimp, top the salad with crabmeat or smoked fish.
⇨ If you have leftover roast chicken or turkey, heat them and top them with hot sweet-and sour-sauce for an almost instant entrée.
⇨ For a simpler meal, omit the salad and the stir-fried peppers; serve the chicken with rice and steamed broccoli or asparagus.

GAME PLAN:

Step 1. Prepare steamed rice.
Step 2. Cut vegetables for stir-fried peppers.
Step 3. Cook chicken.
Step 4. Cook peppers.
Step 5. Make salad.

TIPS:

♥ Mild rice vinegar is a good choice for salad dressings, as you can use more vinegar and less oil.

♥ Sweet-and-sour sauce is a tasty, fat-free preparation.

☺ Instead of chopping garlic and chiles, do what many Chinese do—buy chile paste with garlic.

SHRIMP SALAD
WITH GREENS

2 teaspoons Oriental sesame oil
1 teaspoon vegetable oil
1½ teaspoons rice vinegar
½ teaspoon soy sauce
A few drops Vietnamese or other hot sauce, or to taste
Pepper to taste
1 cup cooked baby shrimp
3 cups romaine lettuce, torn into bite-size pieces
1 cup shredded red cabbage

In a small bowl, whisk sesame oil with vegetable oil, vinegar, soy sauce, hot sauce, and pepper. In another small bowl, add ½ teaspoon dressing to shrimp and mix. Mix lettuce and cabbage in a serving bowl, add remaining dressing, and toss. Serve greens topped with baby shrimp.

Makes 4 servings.

Speedy Sweet-and-Sour Chicken

1¼ *pounds skinless, boneless chicken breasts*
1 *tablespoon vegetable oil*
¼ *cup sugar*
¼ *cup white or red wine vinegar*
¼ *cup ketchup*
¼ *cup soy sauce*
¼ *teaspoon Asian hot sauce, or to taste*
1¼ *teaspoons cornstarch*

Trim visible fat from chicken and cut meat into 1-inch cubes. Heat oil in a heavy sauté pan or wok. Add chicken and sauté over medium heat, stirring, 1 minute. Cover and sauté 3 minutes, stirring once or twice.

Meanwhile, thoroughly mix sugar, vinegar, ketchup, soy sauce, and hot sauce. Add to pan of chicken and mix well. Bring to a simmer. Cover and cook over low heat 5 minutes or until chicken is tender. Chicken is done when color is no longer pink; cut into a thick piece to check.

In small cup, blend cornstarch and 1 tablespoon water. Add to simmering sauce, drizzling it into center of pan. Quickly stir into remaining sauce. Heat until bubbling. Serve hot.

Makes 4 servings.

STEAMED RICE

1⅓ cups long-grain white rice
2⅔ cups water

Bring rice and water to a full boil in a heavy medium saucepan over high heat. Cover and cook over low heat, without stirring, for 15 minutes or until just tender.

Makes 4 servings.

STIR-FRY OF PEPPERS AND GREEN ONION

2 medium red bell peppers
1 medium green bell pepper
4 green onions
1 tablespoon vegetable oil
½ teaspoon Chinese chile paste with garlic, or more to taste
2 teaspoons soy sauce
2 tablespoons chicken broth or water

Cut peppers in strips ½ inch wide. Cut any long pieces in half crosswise. Cut wide end of green onions in half lengthwise, then cut into 1-inch lengths.

Heat oil in a heavy skillet or wok, add peppers, and sauté 2 minutes over high heat. Cover and sauté 4 minutes over medium heat, stirring often. Add chile paste, green onions, soy sauce, and broth. Cover and cook 1 or 2 minutes or until peppers are tender. Serve hot.

Makes 4 servings.

Turkey with
a Tandoori Accent

- *Tandoori turkey* •
- *Basmati rice with peas and cashews* •
- *Steamed zucchini with hot cilantro dressing* •
- *Exotic fruit such as mangoes or Fuji apples* •

AMOUNT OF CALORIES FROM FAT: 25%

These easy-to-prepare specialties of India are perfect for any time of year, but because they are light, the menu is best for summer. Even a brief sojourn in the flavorful tandoori marinade redolent of garlic, ginger, coriander, and cumin transforms lean turkey breasts into a tasty treat and helps prevent them from being dry. If you want to get ahead with the recipe, marinate the turkey overnight—it will gain extra flavor and be more tender. You might also like to have one or two bottled chutneys on the table.

ALTERNATIVES:

⇨ Substitute skinless, boneless chicken breasts for the turkey.
⇨ Use yellow zucchini in summer instead of the green variety, or mix both types.

Game Plan:

Step 1. Prepare marinade; marinate the turkey.
Step 2. Start cooking rice.
Step 3. Make dressing for zucchini.
Step 4. Steam zucchini.
Step 5. Grill or broil turkey.

Tips:

♥ Yogurt-based tandoori marinade is almost fat-free.

① Frozen peas cook with rice—a fast way to add vegetables without an extra pot.

TANDOORI TURKEY

2 large garlic cloves
1 tablespoon coarsely chopped fresh ginger
1 tablespoon vegetable oil
½ cup nonfat plain yogurt
1½ teaspoons ground coriander
1 teaspoon ground cumin
½ teaspoon turmeric
¼ teaspoon cayenne pepper
¼ teaspoon ground cinnamon
½ teaspoon salt
1 pound turkey breast slices, about ¼ inch thick
Lemon wedges

In a mini food processor, process garlic and ginger until finely chopped. Add oil and process to blend. Transfer to a small bowl and stir in yogurt, spices, and salt. Put turkey in a shallow dish and pour marinade over it. Rub marinade into slices. Cover and refrigerate 15 minutes.

Preheat broiler with rack about 3 inches from heat; or heat ridged stovetop grill. Remove turkey from marinade with tongs and set in broiler or on grill. Broil or grill turkey for 2 minutes. Turn over and continue broiling about 2 minutes or until just tender and no longer pink when pierced with a sharp knife; do not overcook. Serve with lemon wedges.

Makes 4 servings.

BASMATI RICE WITH PEAS AND CASHEWS

1 tablespoon vegetable oil
½ cup chopped onion
1½ cups white Basmati rice, rinsed and drained (see Note)
3 cups hot water
Salt and freshly ground pepper to taste
1 cup frozen peas
8 toasted cashews or almonds, for garnish

Heat oil in a large saucepan over medium heat. Add onion and sauté 3 minutes. Add rice and sauté, stirring, 1 minute. Pour hot water over rice and stir once. Add salt and pepper. Bring to boil over high heat. Reduce heat to low, cover tightly, and simmer, without stirring, 12 minutes.

Scatter peas over top of rice in 1 layer. Cover and simmer 3 to 5 minutes, or until rice and peas are tender and liquid is absorbed. Fluff rice gently with a fork. Taste and adjust seasoning. Serve garnished with cashews.

Makes 4 servings.

Note: If you use regular long-grain rice, you do not need to rinse it.

STEAMED ZUCCHINI WITH HOT CILANTRO DRESSING

1¼ pounds zucchini
2 tablespoons vegetable oil
1 tablespoon strained fresh lemon juice
¼ teaspoon Asian or other bottled hot sauce
Salt and freshly ground pepper
1 tablespoon chopped cilantro

Halve zucchini lengthwise, set cut side down, and halve lengthwise again. Cut each piece in half crosswise. In a small bowl, whisk oil with lemon juice, hot sauce, and salt and pepper to taste.

Bring at least 1 inch of water to a boil in base of steamer. Boiling water should not reach holes in steamer rack. Place zucchini on steamer rack above boiling water. Sprinkle with salt, cover tightly, and steam about 5 minutes or until just tender. Stir once or twice. Transfer zucchini to a shallow serving dish. Stir dressing, spoon it over zucchini, and sprinkle with cilantro.

Makes 4 servings.

Turkey Dinner from the Pacific Rim

- *Thai turkey with mint and peppers* •
- *Rice noodles with Chinese vegetables* •
- *Pineapple with melon balls and rum syrup* •

——————— AMOUNT OF CALORIES FROM FAT: 22% ———————

This menu, featuring Pacific Rim flavors, is for people with adventurous tastes. The main course of turkey with red bell peppers, onions, and chiles is slightly hot, but the chiles' heat is balanced by the fresh taste of mint. Remove the seeds from the chiles if you want to tone down their fire. Serve the turkey garnished with the chile halves, but warn everyone that they are hot! Plain steamed rice can accompany the turkey, but thin rice noodles, the Asian counterpart of angel-hair pasta, provide a pleasant change of pace. Have a bottle of Oriental hot sauce on the table in case anyone would like hotter turkey or noodles.

ALTERNATIVES:

⇨ Substitute chicken breasts for turkey.
⇨ Prepare Basmati Rice with Peas and Cashews (page 47) instead of the rice noodles.

GAME PLAN:

Step 1. Boil water for cooking noodles.
Step 2. Cut all ingredients; mince garlic for both recipes.
Step 3. Cook noodles and drain.
Step 4. Prepare turkey dish.
Step 5. Finish noodle dish.
Step 6. Prepare dessert.

TIPS:

♥ Rice noodles can be flavored with chicken broth. They absorb the broth and acquire a rich taste and moist texture, so that only a little oil is needed—and they cook in less than 2 minutes!

⚠ Markets now sell peeled fresh pineapple, diced or in rings. It's a boon to cooks in a hurry, when there's no time to peel a pineapple.

THAI TURKEY WITH MINT AND PEPPERS

1 pound turkey breast slices
2 tablespoons vegetable oil
1 large onion, halved lengthwise and cut into thin lengthwise slices
½ medium red bell pepper, cut in ½-inch strips, then halved crosswise
2 fresh jalapeño or serrano peppers, halved lengthwise
⅓ cup canned chicken broth
3 large garlic cloves, minced
2 tablespoons soy sauce
1 cup fresh mint leaves

Cut turkey in 3 × ¼ × ½-inch strips; set aside. Heat 1 tablespoon oil in a large skillet or wok. Add onion, bell pepper, and hot peppers and sauté over medium-high heat, stirring, 3 minutes. Add 2 tablespoons broth, cover, and cook over medium heat about 3 minutes or until onion browns lightly; it may still be a bit crunchy. Transfer to a bowl.

Add 1 tablespoon oil to skillet. Add turkey and sauté over medium-high heat 1 minute. Add pepper mixture, garlic, remaining broth, and soy sauce to skillet and bring to a boil. Cover and cook over low heat 2 minutes or until turkey is cooked through; cut to check that its color is no longer pink inside. Add mint leaves and cook ½ minute. Serve hot.

Makes 4 servings.

RICE NOODLES WITH CHINESE VEGETABLES

1 (6-ounce) package thin rice noodles or rice sticks (**mai fun**)
1 tablespoon vegetable oil
3 large garlic cloves, minced
½ cup chicken broth
1 cup snow peas (3 ounces), ends removed
2 tablespoons soy sauce
½ teaspoon Asian hot sauce, or to taste
1 (8-ounce) can sliced water chestnuts, drained
1 (5½-ounce) can baby corn, drained, halved if long
1 teaspoon Oriental sesame oil

Add rice noodles to a large pan of boiling water and cook 1½ minutes, lifting noodles with tongs to separate them as they cook. Drain in strainer.

Heat vegetable oil in a large sauté pan, add garlic, and sauté about 15 seconds or until golden. Add broth and bring to a boil. Add snow peas and cook 1 minute. Add soy sauce, hot sauce, water chestnuts, and corn and heat through. Add rice noodles and toss. Add sesame oil and toss well. Serve hot.

Makes 4 servings.

FAYE LEVY

PINEAPPLE WITH MELON BALLS AND RUM SYRUP

2 cups diced fresh pineapple (12-ounce package)
1 tablespoon rum
1 tablespoon sugar
2 cups cantaloupe or honeydew melon balls or dice, or 1 cup of
* each*

Reserve 1 tablespoon juice from pineapple and mix it with rum and sugar in a small cup. Mix fruit. Pour dressing over fruit and mix gently. Serve cold.

Makes 4 servings.

CHAPTER 3

SEAFOOD MENUS

Easy and Elegant Salmon Dinner

• *Classic American dinner salad* •
• *Roasted salmon with coriander and lemon* •
• *Ginger-scented broccoli* •
• *Crisp baguette or Italian sesame bread* •
• *Apples, tangerines, or peaches* •

AMOUNT OF CALORIES FROM FAT: 30%

Prepare this dinner instead of going to a seafood restaurant. It will cost less and probably take less time to get on your table than it does to go to the restaurant and wait to be served. For the main course, roast the salmon briefly at high temperature. It cooks as quickly as grilled salmon and has an added advantage—you don't have to turn it over during cooking. A good additional accompaniment is a microwave "baked" potato, which can be cooking while the salmon is baking. You can top it with nonfat sour cream or a tiny sliver of butter. Instead of fruit for dessert, you might like to serve Grand Canyon Apple Crumble (page 140) in winter, Nectarines in Red Wine (page 69) in summer, or Chocolate Pecan Brownies (page 177) anytime.

ALTERNATIVES:

⇨ Substitute sea bass or Hawaiian escolar fillet for the salmon.
⇨ For a quicker menu, omit the broccoli and serve Spinach Salad with Bell Peppers and Herb Dressing (page 72).

GAME PLAN:

Step 1. Preheat oven. Put salmon in baking dish and add seasonings.
Step 2. Boil water for broccoli. Prepare Chinese dressing for broccoli.
Step 3. Roast salmon.
Step 4. Cook broccoli and add dressing.
Step 5. Make salad.

TIPS:

♥ Sprinkle salmon, a rich fish, only lightly with oil before roasting.

① Salmon fillet is a fast-cooking cut. In some markets you can buy it without its skin.

① Buy "broccoli crowns," which are mostly florets with no thick stalk; or buy ready-to-eat fresh broccoli florets.

CLASSIC AMERICAN DINNER SALAD

4 cups iceberg lettuce mix, romaine lettuce, or a mixture of both
1 cup spinach leaves
1 tablespoon vegetable oil
½ tablespoon wine vinegar
¼ teaspoon dried oregano
Salt and freshly ground pepper
1 large tomato, sliced
6 black olives, halved

Mix lettuce and spinach in a large bowl. Whisk oil, vinegar, and oregano in a small bowl. Add dressing, salt, and pepper to greens and toss thoroughly. Serve topped with tomato slices and olives.

Makes 4 servings.

ROASTED SALMON WITH CORIANDER AND LEMON

1¼ pounds salmon fillet, preferably tail section, about 1 inch thick
1 tablespoon strained fresh lemon juice
2 teaspoons extra-virgin olive oil
1 teaspoon ground coriander
½ teaspoon ground cumin
Salt and freshly ground pepper
Lemon wedges, for serving

Preheat the oven to 450°F. Set fish in a heavy roasting pan. Sprinkle fish with lemon juice and oil and rub them over fish. Sprinkle fish with coriander and cumin, and rub in spices lightly. Then sprinkle fish evenly with salt and pepper.

Roast fish in oven about 10 minutes; fish should just flake and have changed color in thickest part. Serve with lemon wedges.

Makes 4 servings.

GINGER-SCENTED BROCCOLI

1 teaspoon finely grated fresh ginger
2 tablespoons soy sauce
2 tablespoons rice vinegar
1 teaspoon sugar
1½ tablespoons vegetable oil
Freshly ground pepper to taste
2 quarts medium broccoli florets

In a small bowl, mix grated ginger, soy sauce, vinegar, sugar, 1½ tablespoons water, oil, and pepper.

Add broccoli to a large saucepan of boiling salted water and boil uncovered over high heat 3 to 5 minutes or until crisp-tender. Drain well in a colander. Transfer to a shallow serving dish or to plates.

Whisk ginger dressing to blend. Drizzle it over broccoli and serve.

Makes 4 servings.

Springtime Sole

- *Asparagus with citrus dressing* -
- *Sautéed sole with mushrooms, lettuce, and warm vinaigrette* -
- *French bread* -
- *Chocolate-dipped strawberries* -

AMOUNT OF CALORIES FROM FAT: 30%

Celebrate spring with asparagus with orange, lemon, and olive oil dressing—a classic French combination with a Mediterranean tang. For a main course, lightly sauté sole fillets, then cover them with sliced mushrooms cooked with garlic. Make the sauce by adding tarragon vinegar to the pan to blend with any oil left from sautéing the fish and mushrooms. Chocolate-dipped strawberries might seen a surprise in a low-fat dinner, but this treat is right at home in a nutrition-conscious meal. Only a thin layer of chocolate adheres to the strawberry, and you're eating mostly fruit.

ALTERNATIVES:

⇨ Substitute sea bass fillets for the sole.

⇨ Serve steamed rice or boiled potatoes with the sole instead of or in addition to the bread.

⇨ Summer Berry Salad with Framboise (page 79) makes a leaner alternative to the chocolate-dipped strawberries.

GAME PLAN:

Step 1. Trim asparagus.
Step 2. Chop garlic and parsley for sole recipe.
Step 3. Prepare dressing for asparagus.
Step 4. Cook asparagus.
Step 5. Cook sole.
Step 6. Rinse strawberries. Melt chocolate.

TIPS:

♥ When dipping fruit, be sure the chocolate is warm enough so that each piece of fruit receives only a thin coating.

☉ Choose thin asparagus, which does not require peeling and cooks in only 2 minutes.

☉ Turn the strawberries into a tabletop dessert: Melt chocolate during dinner. Bring melted chocolate to the table, so each person can dip his or her own strawberries.

ASPARAGUS WITH CITRUS DRESSING

1 tablespoon extra-virgin olive oil
2 teaspoons fresh orange juice
1 teaspoon fresh lemon juice
Salt and freshly ground pepper
Cayenne pepper to taste
1¼ pounds thin asparagus

Combine olive oil, orange juice, lemon juice, salt, pepper, and cayenne in a bowl. Whisk to combine. Taste and adjust seasoning. Dressing will be tangy.

Cut asparagus spears into 3 pieces, discarding tough ends. Boil asparagus uncovered in a medium saucepan of boiling salted water until just tender when pierced with a small sharp knife, about 2 or 3 minutes. Drain, rinse briefly with cold water, and drain well.

Put asparagus in a shallow serving dish and toss with dressing. Taste and adjust seasoning. Serve warm or at room temperature.

Makes 4 servings.

SAUTÉED SOLE WITH MUSHROOMS, LETTUCE, AND WARM VINAIGRETTE

1 large garlic clove, minced
⅓ cup firmly packed parsley sprigs
1¼ pounds sole or flounder fillets
Salt and freshly ground pepper
2 tablespoons olive oil
1 (6-ounce) package sliced mushrooms (3 cups)
1 quart butter lettuce or mixed baby lettuces
2 tablespoons tarragon vinegar mixed with 1 tablespoon water

Mince garlic in a mini food processor, then the parsley; there is no need to rinse the processor in between.

Sprinkle fish with salt and pepper. Heat 1½ tablespoons oil in a large heavy nonstick skillet over medium-high heat. Add fillets and sauté 2 minutes on each side; if oil begins to brown, reduce heat to medium. Put fish pieces on 4 plates.

Add remaining ½ tablespoon oil to pan and heat it over medium-high heat. Add mushrooms, salt, pepper, and garlic and sauté, tossing often, until just tender, about 2 minutes. Add parsley and mix well. Spoon mushroom mixture over fish. Add lettuce to plates.

Pour vinegar mixture into hot pan off heat, swirl it around pan, and pour it evenly over fish and lettuce.

Makes 4 servings.

CHOCOLATE-DIPPED STRAWBERRIES

12 large strawberries with stems and leaves, or 20 small or
medium strawberries
2½ ounces bittersweet or semisweet chocolate, chopped

Rinse strawberries, leaving stems on. Pat dry with paper towels. Line a tray with foil or waxed paper.

Melt chocolate in a small deep bowl over hot water set over low heat, stirring often. Remove from pan of water. Cool chocolate, stirring often, until it still flows but is thick enough to stick to berries. Chocolate should feel slightly cooler than body temperature.

Pat a strawberry dry again with paper towels. Dip pointed end of berry in chocolate, so that one-third to one-half of the berry is coated. Gently shake berry and let excess chocolate drip back into bowl. Set berry on prepared tray. Dip remaining berries. If chocolate thickens, set it briefly over hot water so it becomes fluid. Refrigerate berries 15 minutes or until chocolate sets. Carefully lift berries from foil or waxed paper to unstick them; replace on tray. Serve cold.

Makes 4 servings.

Provençal Fish Menu

• *Broiled sea bass with garlic and rosemary* •
• *Saint Tropez tomato salad* •
• *Baguette or other fresh French bread* •
• *Nectarines in red wine* •

———————— AMOUNT OF CALORIES FROM FAT: 22% ————————

The main course for this dinner was inspired by a dish I enjoyed recently at a stylish new Mediterranean restaurant in Los Angeles. We could choose salmon, sea bass, or imported John Dory cooked in the broiler with virgin olive oil, garlic, and rosemary. All three fish were wonderful, as their flavor was gently accented by the seasonings. It was a pleasure to taste fish that wasn't charred and didn't have its fine flavor obscured by smoke. For this recipe I find it worthwhile to ask the fishmonger which fish is freshest that day. This has led to delightful discoveries like Hawaiian opakapaka and escolar as well as Chilean sea bass.

ALTERNATIVES:

⇨ Instead of tomato salad, prepare a Mediterranean salad of diced tomatoes, peppers, cucumbers, and green onions, or a Sliced Vegetable Salad with Capers (page 87). Or, if you prefer a heartier accompaniment, serve Fat-Free Fusilli with Peas and Tomatoes (page 133).

Game Plan:

Step 1. Broil fish.
Step 2. Prepare tomato salad.
Step 3. Prepare dessert.

Tips:

♥ Brush or spray fish with just a few drops of extra-virgin olive oil to add flavor and prevent dryness.

♥ Fruit in red wine, a favorite dessert in France and Italy, is made without fat.

☺ Nectarines do not have to be cooked in the wine; just mix them with the wine and sugar.

BROILED SEA BASS WITH GARLIC AND ROSEMARY

1 medium garlic clove, minced
1 teaspoon minced fresh rosemary, or ¼ teaspoon dried
½ teaspoon dried thyme leaves
Cayenne pepper to taste
1½ tablespoons extra-virgin olive oil
1¼ pounds sea bass or halibut steaks, about 1 inch thick
Salt to taste

Preheat broiler with rack about 4 inches from heat source. Mix garlic, rosemary, thyme, cayenne, and oil. Sprinkle fish lightly with salt. Spoon half the garlic mixture over the fish and rub it in. Arrange on broiler rack. Broil 5 minutes. Turn fish over, sprinkle second side with salt, and rub with remaining garlic mixture. Broil about 4 or 5 more minutes or until fish is just opaque when checked inside with a small knife. Serve hot.

Makes 4 servings.

SAINT TROPEZ
TOMATO SALAD

4 teaspoons extra-virgin olive oil
1½ teaspoons tarragon or herb vinegar
Salt and freshly ground pepper
1 pound ripe tomatoes
8 large leaves fresh basil, cut in thin strips

In a small bowl, whisk oil, vinegar, salt, and pepper.
 Slice tomatoes about ⅜ inch thick. Arrange slices slightly overlapping on a platter. Drizzle with dressing. Sprinkle with salt and pepper, then with basil strips.

Makes 4 servings.

NECTARINES IN RED WINE

1½ cups dry red wine, such as Cabernet Sauvignon
½ cup orange juice
¼ cup sugar
6 ripe nectarines

Mix wine with orange juice, sugar, and ¼ cup water until sugar dissolves. Pour into a glass bowl.

Slice nectarines in wedges and add to wine mixture. Mix gently. Refrigerate 10 minutes or up to 2 hours. Serve cold.

Makes 4 servings.

California Seafood Celebration

> • *Spinach salad with bell peppers and herb dressing* •
> • *Easy scallop and shrimp cioppino* •
> • *Crusty sourdough or Italian bread* •
> • *Soft-serve strawberry sorbet with fresh fruit* •
>
> ——————— AMOUNT OF CALORIES FROM FAT: 20% ———————

Cioppino, the pride of fine California restaurants, is a garlic-scented seafood stew in tomato broth. It is believed to have begun as a crab soup in San Francisco and is derived from an Italian soup. Today almost any shellfish might be featured. When I judged a cioppino contest in which several California chefs competed, I found the variations remarkable. The only ingredients used by all were tomatoes, garlic, and olive oil. Other flavors that entered some pots were porcini mushrooms, thyme, basil, oregano, rosemary, saffron, and even jalapeño peppers, cilantro, and orange juice.

Cioppino is one of the few seafood dishes that can in large part be made ahead, making it perfect for entertaining. Simply cook the tomatoes and other flavorings and refrigerate or freeze this base. Buy the freshest seafood at your market and cook it in the base a short time before serving. Bay scallops, which cook very rapidly, are ideal for quick cioppino. So are cooked shelled shrimp, which require only a brief warming in the broth.

ALTERNATIVES:

⇨ If you don't have red peppers, prepare Green Salad with Smoked Almonds and Balsamic Vinegar (page 124) instead of the spinach salad.

⇨ Use cubes of sea bass or other firm fish fillets in the cioppino instead of scallops.

⇨ Serve cioppino with steamed rice or quick-cooking brown rice for spooning into each bowl.

GAME PLAN:

Step 1. If using frozen scallops or shrimp, remove them from the freezer.

Step 2. Prepare cioppino base.

Step 3. Prepare spinach salad.

Step 4. Cook seafood in base.

Step 5. Prepare dessert just before serving.

TIPS:

♥ Use just enough dressing to lightly moisten the spinach leaves.

① Bay scallops are the fastest-cooking shellfish. If you are using sea scallops, add 1 or 2 minutes to the cooking time.

① Strawberry sorbet can be made almost instantly in the food processor from frozen strawberries, without an ice cream machine.

SPINACH SALAD WITH
BELL PEPPERS
AND HERB DRESSING

½ medium red bell pepper
½ medium yellow bell pepper
6 cups spinach leaves, medium packed
1½ tablespoons extra-virgin olive oil
2¼ teaspoons herb or tarragon vinegar
¼ teaspoon dried thyme
Salt and freshly ground pepper

Cut peppers in strips about ⅓ inch wide; cut in half if long. Combine with spinach in a large bowl.

In a small bowl, whisk oil with vinegar and thyme. Toss with spinach and bell peppers. Season to taste with salt and pepper.

Makes 4 servings.

EASY SCALLOP AND SHRIMP CIOPPINO

1½ tablespoons olive oil
1 large onion, sliced thin
2 large garlic cloves, chopped
1 (28-ounce) can diced tomatoes, with juice
1 (8-ounce) can tomato sauce
¾ cup dry red wine, such as Cabernet Sauvignon
½ cup bottled clam juice or thawed frozen fish stock
Salt and freshly ground pepper
Hot pepper sauce to taste
1 pound bay scallops, rinsed
1 teaspoon dried oregano
½ pound cooked large shrimp
1 or 2 tablespoons chopped fresh parsley (optional)

In a large heavy saucepan, heat oil, add onion, and sauté over medium-high heat, stirring often, 3 minutes. Stir in garlic, then tomatoes and their juice, tomato sauce, wine, and clam juice. Cover and bring to a boil. Simmer over medium-low heat 7 minutes. Season to taste with salt, pepper, and hot pepper sauce.

Add scallops and oregano to simmering sauce. Cover and simmer over low heat 2 minutes or until just tender. Add shrimp and heat through, about ½ minute. Serve cioppino in wide bowls. Sprinkle with parsley.

Makes 4 servings.

SOFT-SERVE STRAWBERRY SORBET WITH FRESH FRUIT

1 (1-pound) package frozen strawberries
¼ cup hot water
6 tablespoons sugar
1½ teaspoons strained fresh lemon juice
Any of following fruits for serving: 2 cups blackberries; 4
*   sliced Asian pears; 4 sliced bananas; 4 nectarines or peaches,*
*   cut in wedges*

Puree the strawberries and hot water in a food processor until berries are smooth. Add sugar and lemon juice and process just until well blended. Serve at once or freeze up to 30 minutes.

Serve scoops of sorbet surrounded by fresh fruit.

Makes 4 servings.

Variation: For strawberry sauce, thaw sorbet mixture overnight in refrigerator; or microwave briefly, stirring often, just until thawed.

Summer Salad Feast

- *Crab with couscous, mint, and toasted pine nuts* •
- *Mediterranean chopped salad* •
- *Crisp Italian bread* •
- *Summer berry salad with framboise* •

AMOUNT OF CALORIES FROM FAT: 28%

This menu makes use of the fastest "cooking" technique of all—no cooking! Couscous, a precooked grainlike pasta, has to steep for only a few minutes in hot water. When tossed with crabmeat or other seafood, chopped fresh mint, lemon juice, and a drizzle of olive oil, it becomes a delectable warm-weather entrée and is a favorite of the students in my cooking classes. Serve it with a colorful salad of diced tomatoes and cucumbers, popular throughout the eastern Mediterranean. For dessert you can make the raspberry and blueberry salad even more festive by topping it with raspberry sorbet or vanilla frozen yogurt.

ALTERNATIVES:

⇨ If fresh crabmeat is not available, use frozen. Instead of crabmeat, you can prepare the salad with cooked shrimp or lobster, cooked or canned salmon, canned tuna, smoked fish, or barbecued cod. You can also use imitation crab (surimi, or sealegs), which is found at many supermarkets.

GAME PLAN:

Step 1. Prepare couscous salad.
Step 2. Make chopped salad.
Step 3. Make fruit salad.

TIPS:

♥ In Mediterranean countries, chopped salad is sometimes made without any oil; try it for a fat-free variation.

☉ Steep frozen peas in boiling water along with the couscous. They'll thaw and be tender.

CRAB WITH COUSCOUS, MINT, AND TOASTED PINE NUTS

¼ cup pine nuts or slivered almonds
1 cup couscous
1 cup frozen peas
3 tablespoons strained fresh lemon juice
2 tablespoons extra-virgin olive oil
Salt and freshly ground pepper
¾ pound crabmeat, picked over, any shell and cartilage
    discarded
¼ cup minced fresh mint leaves
Cayenne pepper to taste

Preheat toaster oven or oven to 350°F. Toast pine nuts in oven about 3 minutes or until lightly browned. Transfer to a plate.

Meanwhile, put couscous in a medium saucepan. Shake pan to spread couscous in an even layer. Top with frozen peas. Pour 1½ cups boiling water evenly over mixture and return to boil over high heat. Immediately cover pan tightly and let stand for 7 minutes. Transfer mixture to a bowl. Fluff with fork. Let cool.

Whisk lemon juice with oil in a small bowl. Add salt and pepper to taste. Drizzle dressing over couscous and mix gently with a fork. Add crab, mint, and cayenne and toss salad gently. Taste and adjust seasoning. *Salad can be kept, covered, 1 day in refrigerator.* Serve sprinkled with pine nuts.

Makes 4 servings.

MEDITERRANEAN
CHOPPED SALAD

½ long (European) cucumber, or 1 medium regular cucumber
8 ripe plum tomatoes, or 4 medium tomatoes, cut in small dice
2 green onions, chopped
1 tablespoon extra-virgin olive oil
1 to 2 teaspoons strained fresh lemon juice
Salt and freshly ground pepper

Peel cucumbers if desired and cut into small dice, no larger than ½ inch. In a shallow serving bowl, mix diced tomatoes, cucumber, and green onions. Add oil, lemon juice, and salt and pepper to taste.

Makes 4 servings.

SUMMER BERRY SALAD WITH FRAMBOISE

1½ *cups strawberries, quartered lengthwise*
1 *cup raspberries*
1 *cup blackberries or blueberries, or ½ cup of each*
1 *tablespoon plus 1½ teaspoons sugar*
1 *tablespoon plus 1½ teaspoons framboise (clear raspberry*
  brandy)

Combine berries in a serving bowl. Sprinkle with sugar and framboise and mix gently using a rubber spatula. Cover and refrigerate 15 minutes or until ready to serve.

Makes 4 servings.

Spicy Shrimp Dinner, Southwest Style

- *Jicama and red pepper salad* -
- *Quick shrimp in spicy tomato sauce* -
- *Chili potatoes with garlic* -
- *Orange or grapefruit segments or kiwi slices* -

---------------- AMOUNT OF CALORIES FROM FAT: 25% ----------------

The zesty flavors of the American Southwest are great for low-fat cooking because with so much taste, you don't miss the fat. For a delightfully crunchy, colorful appetizer, dress diced jicama and red bell peppers with lemon juice, olive oil, and cayenne pepper. The main course features shrimp cooked in a quick tomato sauce flavored with cumin, thyme, and hot pepper flakes. You can accompany the shrimp with boiled or microwave "baked" potatoes, but chili potatoes with garlic have a lot more zip. To follow this spicy supper, serve cool seasonal fruit or a Pear and Strawberry Salad with Mint and Lemon (page 125).

ALTERNATIVES:

⇨ If jicama is not available, substitute cucumbers.
⇨ Cook scallops in the tomato sauce instead of shrimp.
⇨ Prepare steamed rice (page 42) instead of potatoes.

Game Plan:

Step 1. Boil potatoes.
Step 2. Chop garlic for potatoes and shrimp.
Step 3. Prepare shrimp recipe.
Step 4. Make salad.
Step 5. Sauté potatoes with garlic and chili powder.

Tips:

♥ Instead of frying potatoes, add a zesty flavor to boiled potatoes by heating them with lightly sautéed garlic and chili powder.

☺ If your supermarket sells jicama sticks, dice them for the salad.

☺ Quarter potatoes so they cook faster.

Jicama and Red Pepper Salad

2 cups diced jicama (¾- to 1-inch cubes)
1 large red bell pepper, diced (1-inch cubes)
2 tablespoons chopped fresh parsley
1 tablespoon extra-virgin olive oil
1 tablespoon strained fresh lemon juice
Salt and freshly ground pepper
Cayenne pepper to taste

Mix jicama, red pepper, parsley, olive oil, and lemon juice. Season to taste with salt, pepper, and cayenne.

Makes 4 servings.

QUICK SHRIMP IN SPICY TOMATO SAUCE

2 tablespoons olive oil
4 large garlic cloves, minced
½ teaspoon ground cumin
2 (14½-ounce) cans diced tomatoes, drained, juice reserved
Salt and freshly ground pepper
½ teaspoon dried thyme leaves
¼ teaspoon hot red pepper flakes
1 pound large shrimp (30 to 35), shelled
Salt and freshly ground pepper
3 tablespoons shredded fresh basil, or 1 teaspoon dried

Heat oil in a large sauté pan. Add garlic and sauté 1 minute over low heat. Stir in cumin, then tomatoes and ½ cup of their juice. Add salt, pepper, thyme, and pepper flakes. Bring to a simmer. Cover and cook over low heat 5 minutes.

Add shrimp to sauce, stir, and sprinkle with salt and pepper. Cover and cook over low heat, stirring occasionally, about 3 or 4 minutes or until tender. To check, cut through a thick end of a shrimp; it should be white throughout. Taste and adjust seasoning. Serve sprinkled with fresh basil; if using dried basil, stir it into sauce.

Makes 4 servings.

CHILI POTATOES
WITH GARLIC

1½ pounds boiling or all-purpose potatoes
Salt
1 tablespoon olive oil
2 medium garlic cloves, minced
1 teaspoon chili powder
Freshly ground pepper

Quarter potatoes and put in a saucepan. Cover with water and add salt. Cover and bring to a boil. Simmer over medium heat 12 to 15 minutes or until potatoes are tender. Do not drain.

Heat oil in a skillet or sauté pan, add garlic, and sauté over low heat for ½ minute. Remove from heat and stir in chili powder. With a slotted spoon, add potatoes. Sprinkle with salt and pepper and toss until coated with garlic mixture. Add 3 tablespoons potato cooking water. Remove from heat. Cover and let stand until ready to serve.

Makes 4 servings.

Spanish Shrimp Fiesta

- *Sliced vegetable salad with capers* •
- *Shrimp in red pepper saffron sauce* •
- *Rice with artichokes and garlic* •
- *Peaches, apricots, nectarines, or fresh berries* •

—————— AMOUNT OF CALORIES FROM FAT: 26% ——————

This menu showcases the favorite seasonings of Spain and is lovely for entertaining. Capers and sherry vinegar transform a pretty salad of tomatoes and cucumbers into a festive appetizer. With plum tomatoes, the salad looks best because the slices come out the same size as the cucumber slices. The entrée is an impressive dish that's amazingly easy—the shrimp is poached directly in the saffron, white wine, and red bell pepper sauce. Steamed Rice (page 42) is a suitable accompaniment for the shrimp, but more glamorous is rice pilaf accented with artichokes, garlic, and parsley.

ALTERNATIVES:

⇨ At many supermarkets you have to ask for saffron, as it's kept in a locked cabinet. If you don't have it, add ½ teaspoon paprika and a pinch of cayenne pepper to the sauce.

⇨ Substitute scallops for the shrimp.

⇨ Instead of the rice, prepare couscous or orzo (rice-shaped pasta) according to the package directions.

GAME PLAN:

Step 1. Prepare rice.
Step 2. Prepare shrimp.
Step 3. Prepare salad while rice and shrimp are cooking.

TIPS:

♥ Sauces thickened with potato starch or cornstarch instead of a traditional roux of butter and flour are much leaner.

☺ Use a mini-chopper to rapidly chop garlic and parsley.

SLICED VEGETABLE SALAD WITH CAPERS

5 medium plum tomatoes (about ½ pound), sliced
½ long (European) cucumber, or 1 regular cucumber, sliced
¼ red onion, sliced and separated in slivers
1 tablespoon extra-virgin olive oil
1½ teaspoons sherry vinegar
Salt and freshly ground pepper
2 teaspoons drained capers

Mix tomato, cucumber, and onion slices in a shallow bowl. Whisk oil and vinegar in a small bowl and add to salad. Sprinkle with salt and pepper and toss gently. Sprinkle with capers and serve.

Makes 4 servings.

Shrimp in Red Pepper Saffron Sauce

2 tablespoons olive oil
2 large red bell peppers, cut in ½-inch dice
1 cup dry white wine
1 cup bottled clam juice or homemade or frozen fish stock
¼ teaspoon saffron threads
1 tablespoon potato starch, dissolved in 2 tablespoons water
1 pound large shrimp (30 to 35 shrimp), shelled
Salt and freshly ground pepper
¼ cup chopped green onions

Heat the oil in a large sauté pan, add peppers, and sauté 5 minutes over medium heat. Add wine, clam juice, and saffron and bring to a boil. Cover and simmer 5 minutes over low heat. Stir potato starch mixture to blend. Add it to sauce, stirring constantly. Bring to simmer, stirring.

Add shrimp to sauce, stir, and sprinkle with salt and pepper. Bring to simmer. Cover and cook over low heat 3 to 4 minutes or until they change color. To check whether shrimp are done, cut through a thick end of a shrimp; it should be white throughout. Stir green onions into sauce. Taste and adjust seasoning.

Makes 4 servings.

RICE WITH ARTICHOKES AND GARLIC

1 tablespoon olive oil
2 large garlic cloves, minced
1¼ cups long-grain white rice
2½ cups hot water
Salt and freshly ground pepper to taste
1 (10-ounce) package frozen artichoke hearts
¼ cup chopped fresh parsley

Heat oil in a large sauté pan. Add garlic and sauté over medium heat 15 seconds. Add rice and sauté, stirring, 1 minute.

Pour hot water over rice and stir once. Add salt and pepper. Bring to boil over high heat. Add frozen artichokes and return to a boil. Reduce heat to low, cover tightly, and simmer, without stirring, 18 minutes or until rice is tender and liquid is absorbed. Add parsley and fluff rice gently with a fork. Taste and adjust seasoning.

Makes 4 servings.

CHAPTER 4

VEGETARIAN MENUS

Casual Soup and Salad Supper

> • Corn salad with sun-dried tomatoes
> and dill dressing •
> • Easy green salad with fresh mushrooms
> and walnut oil •
> • Main-course onion and winter squash soup •
> • Whole-wheat or pumpernickel bread •
> • Comice pears or navel oranges •
>
> ——— AMOUNT OF CALORIES FROM FAT: 25% ———

This supper is perfect for winter. Two salads—one of raw greens and one of cooked vegetables—act as a first course.

A great technique for making a hearty main-course soup in minutes is to use the microwave to cook certain vegetables. It is especially useful for delicately sweet, vitamin A–rich winter squash, which otherwise can take a long time to cut and cook. Serve it topped with a dollop of nonfat sour cream or yogurt. For dessert, in addition to fruit, you might like some Chocolate Pecan Brownies (page 177) or Nonfat Cheesecake (page 173).

ALTERNATIVES:

⇨ Instead of making this a vegetarian meal, you can add meat. Mix 1 or 2 cups diced cooked chicken, turkey, or lean roast beef into the corn salad.

⇨ To vary the taste of the green salad with mushrooms, make it with raspberry vinegar.

⇨ Other salads that you can substitute for the green salad are Spinach Salad with Bell Peppers and Herb Dressing (page 72), Mediterranean Chopped Salad (page 78), or Spinach Salad with Orange and Red Onion (page 113).

GAME PLAN:

Step 1. Cook soup—begin sautéing onions; put squash in microwave.
Step 2. Prepare corn salad.
Step 3. Finish soup.
Step 4. Prepare green salad.

TIPS:

♥ Dry-packed sun-dried tomatoes are fat-free and less expensive than those bottled in oil.

♥ Walnut oil is high in polyunsaturated fat and low in saturated fat. Like extra-virgin olive oil, it's delicious and a small amount adds a lot of flavor.

☺ Make a practically instant green salad from packaged greens and boxed sliced mushrooms, so no rinsing or cutting is needed.

FAYE LEVY

Corn Salad with Sun-Dried Tomatoes and Dill Dressing

⅔ cup dry-packed sun-dried tomatoes
1 pound frozen corn (3⅓ cups)
2 celery stalks, cut in thin slices
1 to 2 tablespoons chopped fresh dill, or 1 teaspoon dried
1 tablespoon vegetable oil
½ tablespoon white wine vinegar
Salt and freshly ground pepper

Put sun-dried tomatoes in a bowl. Pour boiling water over to cover them and let stand 4 minutes. Drain tomatoes and cut into slivers ¼ inch wide.

Cook corn 2 to 3 minutes or according to package instructions. Drain well. Combine corn, sun-dried tomatoes, celery, dill, oil, vinegar, and salt and pepper to taste. Mix gently. Serve cold or at room temperature.

Makes 4 servings.

EASY GREEN SALAD WITH FRESH MUSHROOMS AND WALNUT OIL

2 tablespoons walnut oil
1 tablespoon red wine vinegar
Salt and freshly ground pepper
1 cup sliced fresh mushrooms
6 cups mixed green leaf lettuce and escarole, mixed baby lettuce,
  or romaine lettuce, in bite-size pieces

Whisk oil, vinegar, salt, and pepper. In a medium bowl, mix mushrooms with 1 tablespoon vinaigrette. In a serving bowl, toss lettuce with remaining vinaigrette. Taste and adjust seasoning. Serve lettuce topped with mushrooms.

Makes 4 servings.

Main-Course Onion and Winter Squash Soup

1 tablespoon vegetable oil
2 large onions, halved and thinly sliced
2 (14½-ounce) cans vegetable broth
1 cup hot water
1 small butternut squash (about 1¼ pounds)
½ teaspoon ground ginger
Salt and freshly ground pepper

Heat oil in a Dutch oven or large, wide saucepan. Add onions and sauté over medium-high heat about 4 minutes or until beginning to brown. Add broth and hot water, cover, and bring to a boil. Cook 7 minutes over low heat.

Meanwhile, halve squash, cover with plastic wrap, and microwave on high for 7 minutes or until tender. Remove seeds. Scoop out flesh; it will be soft.

Add squash and ginger to soup. Cook over low heat 5 minutes or until vegetables are tender. Season to taste with salt and pepper. Serve hot.

Makes 4 servings.

Greek Vegetarian Dinner

• *Greek salad with feta cheese* •
• *Easy eggplant stew* •
• *Quick brown rice pilaf with green onions* •
• *Fresh figs or grapes* •

—————— AMOUNT OF CALORIES FROM FAT: 29% ——————

The Greek consumption of dairy products is the highest in the world, yet the Mediterranean diet is known as a healthful one. The Greek example shows there's no need to avoid cheese entirely when following a low-fat program. It should be used judiciously, and a superb way is in a green salad.

Eggplant can be suitable for quick, light cooking when quick-braised in a tomato sauce flavored in the Greek style with onions, garlic, and oregano. The stew keeps well, so you can prepare it ahead. Choose fresh eggplants with smooth, shiny skins and no soft spots; old ones can be bitter and their peel can be tough. If your market carries slender Japanese or Chinese eggplants, use them; their peel is more tender. I enjoy serving this meal in late summer and early autumn, when eggplants and tomatoes are at their best.

ALTERNATIVES:

⇨ Instead of Greek salad, prepare Cucumber Salad with Yogurt and Mint (page 143).
⇨ Substitute bulgur wheat for rice, or spoon the eggplant stew over thin noodles.

GAME PLAN:

Step 1. Prepare ingredients for eggplant stew. Use food processor to chop garlic, then onion. While tomatoes and eggplant simmer, wipe processor and chop parsley.

Step 2. Cook eggplant.

Step 3. While eggplant is simmering, prepare rice.

Step 4. Make salad.

TIPS:

♥ Salads need only a little feta cheese for accent, as it is very flavorful. Choose a reduced-fat feta if you like. If you prefer to omit the cheese, the salad will still taste good.

① Pitting olives is time-consuming. Either buy pitted olives or, if using olives with pits, point this out when you serve the salad.

① Quick-cooking or instant brown rice is ready in 10 minutes instead of the usual 45.

GREEK SALAD
WITH FETA CHEESE

1 quart bite-size pieces romaine lettuce
¼ small red onion, thinly sliced, separated into slivers
1½ tablespoons extra-virgin olive oil
2 teaspoons red wine vinegar or lemon juice
Salt and freshly ground pepper
½ teaspoon dried oregano
2 ripe medium tomatoes, cut into wedges
8 pitted black olives
⅓ cup feta cheese, crumbled into bite-size chunks

In a shallow salad bowl, combine lettuce, onion, olive oil, vinegar, salt, pepper, and oregano. Toss well. Top with tomato wedges, olives, and feta cheese.

Makes 4 servings.

EASY EGGPLANT STEW

1 medium eggplant (about 1¼ pounds)
2 tablespoons olive oil
1 medium onion, chopped
4 large garlic cloves, minced
Salt and freshly ground pepper
1 (28-ounce) can diced tomatoes, drained, juice reserved
1 bay leaf
1 teaspoon dried oregano
2 tablespoons chopped fresh parsley (optional)

Cut eggplant into 1 × 1 × ¾-inch dice. In a heavy Dutch oven or large casserole, heat oil, add onion, and sauté over medium heat 2 minutes. Stir in garlic. Add eggplant dice, salt, and pepper and mix well over low heat until eggplant is coated with onion mixture.

Add tomatoes plus ⅓ cup juice, bay leaf, and oregano and cook over high heat, stirring, until bubbling. Cover and simmer over medium-low heat, stirring often, 20 minutes or until eggplant is tender. Discard bay leaf. Taste and adjust seasoning. *Stew can be kept, covered, 3 days in refrigerator.* Serve hot or cold, sprinkled with parsley.

Makes 4 servings.

QUICK BROWN RICE WITH GREEN ONIONS

5 green onions
1 tablespoon olive oil
2 cups quick-cooking brown rice
1 (14½-ounce) can vegetable broth, or 1¾ cups water
Salt and freshly ground pepper

Slice white and light green parts of green onions. Chop dark green parts. Heat oil in a medium saucepan over medium heat. Add white and light green parts of green onion and sauté ½ minute. Add rice and sauté, stirring, ½ minute.

Add broth or water and stir once. Bring to boil over high heat. Reduce heat to low, cover tightly, and simmer, without stirring, 5 minutes. Stir in dark green part of green onions. Cover and let stand 5 minutes. Fluff rice gently with a fork. Season to taste with salt and pepper.

Makes 4 servings.

A Healthy Toast
to the New Year

• *Black-eyed peas with corn and carrots* •
• *Nonfat yogurt* •
• *Garlic-scented spinach* •
• *Red cabbage salad with walnuts and orange* •
• *Multigrain or whole-wheat bread* •
• *McIntosh, Golden Delicious, or Gala apples* •

——————— AMOUNT OF CALORIES FROM FAT: **30%** ———————

Black-eyed peas are a favorite food for the New Year, as they symbolize good luck. Traditional recipes call for cooking them with fatty meats, but when they are prepared in a tasty, low-fat version with carrots, corn, and herbs, they provide a healthful way to begin the year. Serve them with yogurt and accompany with other nutrient-rich vegetables such as spinach and a cheery red cabbage salad. Unlike most other "greens," red cabbage can be mixed with its dressing and kept one or two days, so you can get ahead with preparing this menu if you wish. For dessert, crisp apple slices can be served with Fast Fat-Free Rice Pudding (page 175).

ALTERNATIVES:

⇨ You can use frozen black-eyed peas but their cooking time is longer.

⇨ Vary the black-eyed pea recipe by substituting frozen lima beans.

GAME PLAN:

Step 1. Cook black-eyed peas with carrots.
Step 2. Meanwhile, chop garlic, parsley, and green onions.
Step 3. Cook spinach.
Step 4. Prepare salad.

TIPS:

♥ Use walnut pieces instead of walnut halves in salads, so you have more bites with a walnut taste. If you wish to further reduce the fat, omit the nuts.

☉ Pre-soaked black-eyed peas, which are usually found in bags in the produce section, are the fastest-cooking form of this vegetable. They cook in 15 to 18 minutes.

BLACK-EYED PEAS WITH CORN AND CARROTS

1 *(11-ounce) package pre-soaked black-eyed peas, rinsed*
2 *large carrots, sliced ⅓ inch thick (2 cups)*
1 *(14½-ounce) can vegetable broth*
2 *cups frozen corn*
2 *green onions, chopped*
⅓ *cup chopped fresh parsley*
1 *tablespoon olive oil*
Salt and freshly ground pepper

In a saucepan, combine black-eyed peas, carrots, and broth. Cover and bring to a boil. Cook over medium-low heat 12 minutes. Add corn, cover, and bring to boil. Simmer 3 minutes. Drain; cooking liquid can be saved for soups. Transfer mixture to a serving bowl. Add green onions, parsley, and olive oil and mix well. Season to taste with salt and pepper. Serve hot.

Makes 4 servings.

Garlic-Scented Spinach

2 (10-ounce) packages fresh spinach leaves, rinsed
2 tablespoons olive oil
2 large garlic cloves, minced
Salt and freshly ground pepper
Cayenne pepper to taste

In a Dutch oven, put spinach with the water clinging to its leaves. Cover and cook over medium-high heat, stirring occasionally, 6 minutes or until wilted. Drain in a colander, rinse with cold water, and drain well. Squeeze gently to remove excess water.

Heat oil in same pan over medium heat. Add garlic and sauté 10 seconds. Add spinach and season to taste with salt, pepper, and cayenne. Stir 2 minutes to heat through. Serve hot.

Makes 4 servings.

RED CABBAGE SALAD
WITH WALNUTS
AND ORANGE

4 cups shredded red cabbage
1 celery stalk, sliced thin
1 tablespoon red wine vinegar
2 tablespoons vegetable oil
Salt and freshly ground pepper
¼ cup walnut pieces
1 orange, peeled and divided into segments

Mix cabbage and celery in a large bowl. Add vinegar, oil, salt, and pepper and mix until cabbage is evenly moistened. Taste and adjust seasoning. Serve topped with walnuts and orange segments.

Makes 4 servings.

South-of-the-Border
Vegetarian Meal

• *Avocado, red onion, and romaine salad* •
• *Hot tortillas* •
• *Spicy black beans* •
• *Brown rice with tomatoes and yellow squash* •
• *Pineapple, melon, or papaya* •

AMOUNT OF CALORIES FROM FAT: 24%

Mexican-inspired menus do not require gobs of melted cheese to be tasty. This satisfying, healthful supper begins with a delicious green salad with a tangy lime dressing topped with ripe Haas avocado. The main course of black beans is accented with sautéed onions and bell peppers and spiced with cumin and garlic. Serve it with fast-cooking brown rice with oregano and vegetables. On the table have Fast Fresh Tomato Salsa (page 169), Quick Cilantro Salsa (page 170), or your favorite prepared salsa.

I like to accompany the meal with hot flour tortillas, which can be heated in seconds in the microwave. Buy tortillas made without lard. If you wish, omit the rice and roll the black beans in tortillas to make bean burritos. You might want to munch on jicama sticks along with the meal. They are available prepared at some markets.

ALTERNATIVES:

⇨ Substitute chickpeas (garbanzo beans) for the black beans.

⇨ To add meat to the meal, add 1 or 2 cups diced cooked chicken or turkey to the black beans. Then you might like to omit the avocado from the salad to keep the menu lean.

GAME PLAN:

Step 1. Dice yellow squash for brown rice recipe; prepare onion, peppers, and garlic for black beans recipe.
Step 2. Begin preparing rice (paragraph 1).
Step 3. Begin preparing black beans (paragraph 1).
Step 4. Finish rice.
Step 5. Finish beans.
Step 6. Make salad.

TIPS:

♥ Avocado is rich, but its fat is mostly monounsaturated, the same type that is in olive oil.

♥ Black beans are a good source of protein, have a meaty texture and flavor, and are extremely low in fat.

① At some markets you can buy fresh peeled and even chopped garlic—a real time-saver. Chopped preserved garlic is available in jars, but I prefer the flavor of fresh garlic.

AVOCADO, RED ONION, AND ROMAINE SALAD

½ medium red onion
1 quart bite-size pieces romaine lettuce
2 teaspoons strained fresh lime juice
1 tablespoon extra-virgin olive oil
Salt and freshly ground pepper
Pure chili powder or cayenne pepper to taste
1 small Haas avocado

Cut red onion crosswise into thin half-moons and separate them in slivers. In a salad bowl, mix onion with lettuce, lime juice, olive oil, salt, pepper, and chili powder. Taste and adjust seasoning.

Just before serving, halve the avocado, remove pit, and peel. Cut in slices. Serve salad topped with avocado.

Makes 4 servings.

Spicy Black Beans

1 tablespoon olive oil
1 medium onion, sliced
2 medium green bell peppers, or 1 red and 1 green, cut in ½-inch-
  wide strips
4 large garlic cloves, chopped
1 teaspoon ground cumin
2 (15-ounce) cans black beans, drained
Salt and freshly ground pepper
½ teaspoon hot red pepper flakes, or more to taste
3 tablespoons chopped cilantro (optional)

Heat oil in a medium sauté pan. Add onion and peppers and sauté over medium heat 5 minutes.

Add garlic and cumin and stir over low heat 1 minute. Add beans, ⅓ cup water, salt, pepper, and pepper flakes. Stir and bring to boil. Cover and simmer 5 to 7 minutes or until peppers are tender. Add cilantro if desired. Taste and adjust seasoning. Serve hot.

Makes 4 servings.

BROWN RICE
WITH TOMATOES
AND YELLOW SQUASH

1 tablespoon olive oil
2 medium yellow crookneck squash (8 ounces total), cut in ½-
inch dice
2 cups quick-cooking brown rice
1 (14½-ounce) can diced tomatoes, drained
1 teaspoon dried oregano
Salt and freshly ground pepper

Heat oil in a medium saucepan. Add squash and sauté over medium heat 2 minutes. Add rice and 1¾ cups water and stir once. Bring to a boil over high heat. Reduce heat to low, cover tightly, and simmer, without stirring, 5 minutes.

Lightly stir in tomatoes and oregano and heat to simmer. Cover, remove from heat, and let stand 5 minutes. Fluff rice gently with a fork. Season to taste with salt and pepper.

Makes 4 servings.

North African Winter Menu

• *Spinach salad with orange and red onion* •
• *Cumin-scented chickpeas* •
• *Rice pilaf with pine nuts and roasted peppers* •
• *Winter pears or dessert apples* •

AMOUNT OF CALORIES FROM FAT: 21%

The warm hues and vibrant tastes of this North African menu demonstrate that even in winter you can have a dinner that is colorful and fresh. In spring you can vary the spinach salad with seasonal sweet onions. Chickpeas (garbanzo beans) and other dried beans benefit greatly from being seasoned with cumin, as in the Algerian-style main dish. Briefly simmering the beans in a garlicky, spicy tomato sauce gives them an enticing aroma. You can add the amount of harissa, or other hot pepper sauce you prefer, to make the beans mild-tasting or fiery hot. For dessert, accompany the fruit, if you wish, with Honey-Yogurt Sauce (page 135).

ALTERNATIVES:

⇨ Prepare salad using romaine lettuce instead of spinach.
⇨ Instead of green salad, begin with a cool Cucumber Salad with Yogurt and Mint (page 143); or serve the chickpeas and rice with lightly cooked broccoli florets.
⇨ Use canned white beans, such as Great Northern beans, instead of chickpeas.
⇨ Serve beans with couscous, bulgur wheat, or fresh pita bread instead of rice.

Game Plan:

Step 1. Toast nuts and cook rice.
Step 2. Prepare chickpea dish.
Step 3. Cut peppers and parsley; add to rice.
Step 4. Make salad.

Tips:

♥ Chickpeas are rich-tasting, so only a little oil is needed in their sauce.

○ Use canned, diced tomatoes instead of whole ones to make faster, easier tomato sauce.

SPINACH SALAD WITH ORANGE AND RED ONION

4 cups spinach leaves
¼ medium red onion, sliced thin and separated into slivers
1 tablespoon extra-virgin olive oil
½ tablespoon strained fresh lemon juice
Salt and freshly ground pepper
1 medium orange, peeled and sectioned

In a shallow serving bowl, combine spinach, onion, oil, lemon juice, salt, and pepper. Toss to mix well. Taste and adjust seasoning. Serve topped with orange segments.

Makes 4 servings.

CUMIN-SCENTED CHICKPEAS

2 (15-ounce) cans chickpeas (garbanzo beans)
1 tablespoon olive oil
6 large garlic cloves, chopped
1 (28-ounce) can diced tomatoes, drained
2 teaspoons ground cumin
2 teaspoons paprika
Salt to taste
2 tablespoons tomato paste
½ teaspoon harissa or bottled hot sauce, or more to taste (see Note)

Rinse and drain chickpeas. Heat oil in a medium saucepan, add garlic, and sauté 15 seconds over medium heat. Add tomatoes, cumin, paprika, and salt and bring to boil. Simmer uncovered 5 minutes. Add tomato paste and ⅓ cup water and bring to a boil. Add chickpeas and harissa. Simmer uncovered over medium-low heat 3 minutes. Taste and adjust seasoning. *Chickpeas can be kept, covered, 2 days in refrigerator.* Serve hot.

Makes 4 servings.

Note: Harissa is North African hot sauce made of dried red chiles, garlic, and ground coriander.

RICE PILAF WITH PINE NUTS AND ROASTED PEPPERS

¼ cup pine nuts or slivered almonds
1 tablespoon olive oil
1½ cups long-grain white rice
3 cups hot water
Salt and freshly ground pepper to taste
1 cup strips of bottled roasted peppers
¼ cup chopped fresh parsley

Preheat the oven or toaster oven to 350°F. Toast pine nuts in oven 3 minutes or until lightly browned. Remove to a plate.

Heat oil in a large heavy saucepan over medium heat. Add rice and sauté, stirring, 2 minutes. Pour hot water over rice and stir once. Add salt and pepper. Bring to a boil over high heat, reduce heat to low, cover tightly, and simmer, without stirring, 14 minutes or until tender. Fluff rice with a fork and gently stir in peppers and parsley. Taste and adjust seasoning. Serve sprinkled with toasted nuts.

Makes 4 servings.

Minestrone Menu

• *Minestrone in minutes* •

• *Light pesto* •

• *Crusty Italian bread or sesame bread* •

• *Angel food cake à la mode with blueberries
and Grand Marnier* •

AMOUNT OF CALORIES FROM FAT: 18%

It might seem impossible to achieve a savory soup without long simmering, but you can have mouthwatering minestrone in short order by using prepared vegetable broth and rapid-cooking vegetables. In Italy, many versions of minestrone are made without pesto; you can omit it to save time and calories. The soup tastes wonderful on its own, but if you like, serve grated Parmesan cheese on the side; be frugal with it to avoid adding much fat.

If you would like an appetizer, roasted or grilled peppers, either bottled or marinated as on page 167, are a great choice; or set out marinated artichokes or mushrooms from a jar, along with carrot and celery sticks and radishes.

ALTERNATIVES:

⇨ Minestrone can be made with many other vegetables. Vary the recipe with chickpeas (garbanzo beans) or black-eyed peas instead of white beans, 2 or 3 Swiss chard leaves cut in strips instead of spinach, frozen corn or green beans instead of peas, or ready-to-eat pieces of winter squash instead of carrots.

⇨ Although we are most familiar with minestrone made solely of vegetables, meat is added in some regions of Italy. Stir in 1 or 2 cups cooked chicken or turkey if you like.

⇨ If you have cooked rice on hand, heat it in a covered bowl in the microwave. Omit the noodles and top each serving of minestrone with ½ cup hot rice.

⇨ If you prefer a simpler dessert, double the blueberry and Grand Marnier mixture and present it as a fruit salad, without cake or frozen yogurt.

GAME PLAN:

Step 1. Chop onion in food processor.

Step 2. While simmering mixture in first paragraph of minestrone recipe, cut remaining ingredients.

Step 3. Prepare pesto while soup simmers.

Step 4. Prepare blueberry-Grand Marnier mixture for dessert.

Step 5. Assemble dessert at serving time.

TIPS:

♥ Angel food cake is fat-free and is a terrific base for fruit and ice cream desserts.

☉ When buying grated Parmesan instead of grating your own, choose it from the refrigerated cheese section rather than from the dry-goods shelf so it will be fresher.

MINESTRONE IN MINUTES

1 tablespoon olive oil
1 large onion, chopped
2 (14½-ounce) cans vegetable broth
1 medium carrot, diced (about 1 cup)
1 cup thin soup noodles
2 small zucchini, diced
½ cup frozen peas
1 cup torn spinach leaves
1 (15-ounce) can white beans, such as Great Northern, drained
1 (28-ounce) can diced tomatoes, drained
Salt and freshly ground pepper

Heat oil in a large saucepan, add onion, and sauté 3 minutes over medium-high heat. Reserve 3 tablespoons vegetable broth for pesto recipe. Add carrot, remaining broth, and 2 cups water to onions. Cover and bring to boil. Cook over medium-low heat 7 minutes.

Add noodles and bring to a boil. Add zucchini, peas, spinach, beans, and tomatoes. Cover and bring to a boil. Cook over medium heat 3 minutes or until vegetables and noodles are tender. Season to taste with salt and pepper.

Makes 4 servings.

LIGHT PESTO

2 large garlic cloves, peeled
1 tablespoon pine nuts or walnuts
1 cup (medium packed) fresh basil leaves
2 tablespoons grated Parmesan cheese
1 tablespoon extra-virgin olive oil
3 tablespoons canned vegetable broth

With the blade of a food processor turning, drop garlic cloves, 1 at a time, through feed tube and process until finely chopped. Add nuts, basil, and cheese. Process until basil is chopped. With blade turning, add olive oil, then broth. Scrape down sides and process until mixture is well blended. Transfer to a small bowl and set aside. *Pesto can be kept, covered, 1 day in refrigerator. Bring to room temperature before using.*

Makes about ⅓ cup, about 4 servings.

Angel Food Cake à la Mode with Blueberries and Grand Marnier

2 cups blueberries
1 tablespoon sugar
2 tablespoons Grand Marnier
4 slices angel food cake
4 scoops vanilla frozen yogurt, ice milk or light ice cream

In a bowl, mix blueberries with sugar and Grand Marnier.

On each plate, set a slice of angel food cake and top it with a scoop of frozen yogurt. Spoon blueberry mixture over and around the cake.

Makes 4 servings.

CHAPTER 5

PASTA MENUS

Summer Brunch with Italian Flavors

- *Pasta and roast beef salad with garlic and tomatoes* •
- *Green salad with smoked almonds and balsamic vinegar* •
- *Pear and strawberry salad with mint and lemon* •

AMOUNT OF CALORIES FROM FAT: **29%**

This salad menu is simple to serve and is ideal for family meals or for entertaining. Pasta salads are an American creation, but they have evolved far beyond the sweet-and-sour mayonnaise-dressed macaroni salads sold at supermarkets. Today pasta salads often make use of Italian seasonings, as in the main-course salad of pasta shells and roast beef with a garlic-oregano dressing. Pair the entrée with an easy-to-prepare salad of spinach and lettuce topped with smoked almonds. If you would like an additional accompaniment, Asparagus with Citrus Dressing (page 62) is an excellent choice. For dessert, you can top the fruit salad with strawberry sorbet. If you prefer a more substantial dessert, try cheesecake made with nonfat ricotta (page 173).

ALTERNATIVES:

⇨ Substitute roasted or smoked turkey for the beef.
⇨ Use fusilli instead of pasta shells.
⇨ Use other smoked or toasted nuts in the green salad instead of smoked almonds. Or prepare Red Cabbage Salad with Tarragon Dressing (page 134) instead of green salad.

GAME PLAN:

Step 1. Boil water for pasta.
Step 2. Prepare pasta salad.
Step 3. Make green salad.
Step 4. Make fruit salad.

TIPS:

♥ Equal amounts of lemon juice and sugar make a tasty, fat-free dressing for fruit salads.

☺ For pasta salads, buy roast beef from a deli or use leftover lean roast beef from a previous meal.

☺ To save time, you can substitute blackberries or raspberries for strawberries, as there are no green caps to remove.

PASTA AND ROAST BEEF SALAD WITH GARLIC AND TOMATOES

2 tablespoons extra-virgin olive oil
1 tablespoon wine vinegar
1 small garlic clove, minced
Salt and freshly ground pepper to taste
1 teaspoon dried oregano leaves, crumbled
1½ cups (6 ounces) strips of lean roast beef (½ × ½ × ⅛ inch)
8 ounces ripe tomatoes, diced
3¾ cups medium pasta shells (9 ounces)

In a large bowl, combine oil, vinegar, garlic, salt, pepper, and oregano. Add beef and tomatoes and mix well.

Cook pasta uncovered in a large pot of boiling salted water over high heat, stirring occasionally, about 8 minutes or until tender but firm to the bite. Drain and add to tomato mixture. Mix well. Taste and adjust seasoning. Serve warm or cold; if serving cold, remove from refrigerator about 15 minutes before serving.

Makes 4 servings.

GREEN SALAD
WITH SMOKED ALMONDS
AND BALSAMIC VINEGAR

2 cups iceberg lettuce mix
2 cups spinach leaves
1 tablespoon extra-virgin olive oil
1½ teaspoons balsamic vinegar
Salt and freshly ground pepper
¼ cup smoked or toasted almonds, coarsely chopped

In a salad bowl, toss lettuce with spinach, oil, vinegar, salt, and pepper. Taste and adjust seasoning. Serve sprinkled with almonds.

Makes 4 servings.

PEAR AND STRAWBERRY SALAD WITH MINT AND LEMON

1 tablespoon lemon juice
1 tablespoon sugar
2 ripe medium pears
2 cups strawberries, caps removed and quartered lengthwise
1½ tablespoons chopped fresh mint

In a small cup, mix lemon juice and sugar. Halve and core pears and cut into 12 lengthwise wedges. In a shallow serving bowl, gently mix pears with strawberries. Add lemon dressing and mix gently. Serve cold, sprinkled with mint.

Makes 4 servings.

Old-Fashioned Spaghetti Supper

- *Italian salad with artichoke hearts and chickpeas* •
- *Italian sesame bread* •
- *Spaghetti with mushroom meat sauce* •
- *Frozen yogurt with dark chocolate sauce* •

——————— AMOUNT OF CALORIES FROM FAT: 26% ———————

For supper on a cold winter night, many of us crave hearty, warming dishes like pasta topped with a thick, meaty, old-fashioned spaghetti sauce. Most traditional recipes call for at least an hour of cooking so the sauce becomes thick. Yet spaghetti sauce can be prepared in just a few minutes, since that is all the time required to cook ground meat. When you add only a small quantity of liquid, the sauce thickens quickly. I prefer the taste of briefly cooked spaghetti sauces, as the meat retains its flavor and does not turn into bits of dry, over-cooked meat. Spaghetti sauces make sense nutritionally and economically because a small amount of beef gives a satisfying meat taste. The sauce can be refrigerated for a day or two or can be frozen.

ALTERNATIVES:

⇨ Instead of beef, prepare sauce with lean ground lamb, chicken, or turkey. Meaty mushroom sauce is also a fine accompaniment for orzo or rice. Shell-shaped and spiral pastas also are superb partners for the sauce because they hold the small morsels of meat and make it easy to savor the pasta with the sauce.

⇨ To round out the quick winter menu, you might like to serve a briefly cooked green vegetable, such as fresh or frozen spinach, broccoli, zucchini, green beans, or snow peas, alongside the spaghetti or mixed into the sauce.

⇨ If you prefer to follow the pasta with a fruit dessert, serve Grand Canyon Apple Crumble (page 140) or a navel orange and banana salad with a splash of Grand Marnier.

GAME PLAN:

Step 1. Boil water for spaghetti.
Step 2. Mince garlic in food processor, add onion, and mince together.
Step 3. Make spaghetti sauce; meanwhile, cook spaghetti.
Step 4. Make chocolate sauce.
Step 5. Make salad.

TIPS:

♥ Drain artichokes well from the oil-enriched marinade.

♥ Make spaghetti sauces with extra-lean ground beef, now available with only 7 percent fat.

ⓘ Marinated vegetables—artichokes, mushrooms, and peppers—are easy to find in jars and are a tasty addition to salads.

ITALIAN SALAD WITH ARTICHOKE HEARTS AND CHICKPEAS

4 cups bite-size pieces romaine lettuce
1 (8¾-ounce) can chickpeas (garbanzo beans)
1½ tablespoons olive oil
1 tablespoon lemon juice
½ teaspoon dried oregano
Salt and freshly ground pepper
4 pieces marinated artichokes (quarters)
2 medium tomatoes, cut into wedges

In a shallow serving bowl, toss lettuce with chickpeas, oil, lemon juice, and oregano. Season to taste with salt and pepper. Serve salad topped with artichoke pieces and tomato wedges.

Makes 4 servings.

SPAGHETTI WITH MUSHROOM MEAT SAUCE

2 large garlic cloves, minced
1 medium onion, minced
1 tablespoon olive oil
½ pound (about 1 cup) extra-lean ground beef (7% fat)
1 (14½-ounce) can diced tomatoes, drained
2 tablespoons tomato paste
½ cup canned beef broth
1 teaspoon dried basil
½ teaspoon hot red pepper flakes
Salt and freshly ground pepper
1 (6-ounce) package sliced mushrooms (about 3 cups)
1 pound spaghetti

Chop garlic in food processor, add onion, and chop together. Heat oil in a heavy medium sauté pan. Add onion mixture and sauté over medium-high heat, stirring often, 2 minutes. Add beef and sauté, crumbling meat with a fork, about 3 minutes or until it changes color.

Add tomatoes, tomato paste, broth, basil, pepper flakes, salt, and pepper and bring to a boil, stirring. Add mushrooms. Cover and cook over medium-low heat, stirring occasionally, 8 to 10 minutes.

Meanwhile, cook spaghetti in a large pot of boiling salted water 8 to 10 minutes, or until tender but firm to the bite. Drain and transfer to a large heated bowl. Add sauce and toss. Taste and adjust seasoning. Serve hot.

Makes 4 to 6 servings.

FROZEN YOGURT WITH DARK CHOCOLATE SAUCE

½ cup nonfat milk
⅓ cup semisweet chocolate chips
¼ cup unsweetened cocoa
¼ cup brown sugar
1 teaspoon vanilla extract
4 to 8 scoops vanilla, strawberry, or coffee frozen yogurt or ice milk

In a small saucepan, bring milk to a boil. Remove from heat and add chocolate chips. Whisk until smooth. Whisk in cocoa and brown sugar. Bring to a simmer. Cook over low heat 2 minutes, stirring constantly, until sugar dissolves and sauce thickens slightly. Remove from heat. Add vanilla. Serve immediately or refrigerate.

If sauce is cold, reheat briefly in microwave, stirring often, or in a bowl set in a pan of hot water over low heat.

Serve 2 tablespoons sauce per serving; pour it over frozen yogurt or ice milk.

Makes 4 servings.

Colorful Summer Supper

• *Fat-free fusilli with peas and tomatoes* •
• *Red cabbage salad with tarragon dressing* •
• *Fruit with honey-yogurt sauce* •

AMOUNT OF CALORIES FROM FAT: 10%

This is the fastest and easiest menu in the book and one of the lowest in fat as well—only 10 percent of its calories are from fat. The colorful main course is practically effortless, has only three ingredients, and is made without any oil or other fats. For best flavor, use the finest quality pasta available. Serve the pasta with a healthful red cabbage salad that's ready in seconds. For dessert, dip fruit in a quick vanilla-accented sauce of honey and yogurt. I love whole strawberries or slices of peaches, nectarines, bananas, pears, or apples with the refreshing sauce.

ALTERNATIVES:

⇨ Use frozen broccoli or mixed frozen vegetables instead of peas.
⇨ Instead of red cabbage salad, prepare Coleslaw with Mustard Dressing (page 22) or Easy Green Salad with Fresh Mushrooms and Walnut Oil (page 94).

GAME PLAN:

Step 1. Boil water for pasta.
Step 2. Prepare salad.
Step 3. Prepare honey-yogurt sauce.
Step 4. Finish pasta dish.
Step 5. Slice fruit.

TIPS:

♥ Pasta prepared without oil tastes great, but be sure to eat it as soon as it is ready.

♥ Use extra-creamy nonfat yogurt for a "creamy" dessert sauce.

☉ Buying shredded red cabbage in packages makes for speedy salads.

FAT-FREE FUSILLI WITH PEAS AND TOMATOES

1 pound fusilli, rotelle, or spiral pasta
3 cups frozen green peas
1 (28-ounce) can diced tomatoes
Salt and freshly ground pepper

Cook pasta uncovered in a large pot of boiling salted water over high heat according to package directions, adding peas 3 minutes before pasta is done. Return to a boil after adding peas and cook 3 minutes or until pasta is tender but firm to the bite.

Drain tomatoes in a large strainer and immediately add pasta mixture, so tomatoes are warmed from heat of pasta. Transfer to a large bowl. Season to taste with salt and pepper and mix well. Serve immediately.

Makes 4 to 6 servings.

RED CABBAGE SALAD
WITH TARRAGON DRESSING

5 cups shredded red cabbage
4 teaspoon vegetable oil
2 teaspoons tarragon vinegar
Salt and freshly ground pepper

In a salad bowl, combine cabbage, oil, and vinegar. Mix well. Season to taste with salt and pepper.

Makes 4 servings.

FRUIT WITH HONEY-YOGURT SAUCE

1 cup nonfat yogurt, preferably extra-creamy
2 tablespoons honey
1 teaspoon vanilla extract
1 or 2 of the following: 2 to 4 pears, cut in slices; 2 to 4
  bananas, cut in chunks; 2 to 4 oranges, peeled and divided in
  segments; 4 cups whole strawberries

Mix yogurt, honey, and vanilla in a bowl. Arrange fruit on a platter. Serve sauce cold, for dipping fruit.

Makes 4 servings.

Fall Favorites with a New Twist

- *Chili pasta with turkey and lima beans* •
- *Carrots with cranberries and mint* •
- *Grand Canyon apple crumble* •

AMOUNT OF CALORIES FROM FAT: 28%

Turkey and cranberries come together not only for Thanksgiving; they can also be the basis of a speedy and savory pasta menu. Use flavored pasta to help cut fat and save time. Because the pasta already is tasty, a light sauce complements it well.

Serve this colorful entrée with carrots with dried cranberries, a new twist on traditional glazed carrots that also is a delicious partner for grilled poultry or meat. For a superb finale, serve a fast and foolproof version of another American favorite—apple crumble. Instead of making a high-fat pastry, sprinkle the warm, cinnamon-scented apples with granola and top them with your favorite brand of vanilla frozen yogurt. This dessert was inspired by the apple crumble I enjoyed at a restaurant in Arizona, overlooking the Grand Canyon.

ALTERNATIVES:

⇨ Substitute pepper pasta, Cajun pasta, or any other spicy pasta for the chili pasta; or use tomato pasta or plain pasta and add a bit more hot sauce.

⇨ Instead of cooked turkey, use smoked turkey or thin-sliced roast beef, which you can purchase from a deli or at the supermarket's deli department.

⇨ If you have homemade grilled peppers (page 167), use them instead of bottled peppers in the pasta recipe.

GAME PLAN:

Step 1. Heat water to cook pasta.
Step 2. Begin cooking carrots.
Step 3. Cut vegetables for pasta dish.
Step 4. Cook apples for dessert.
Step 5. Finish carrots.
Step 6. Finish pasta.
Step 7. Assemble dessert at serving time.

TIPS:

♥ Make glazed carrots with a little vegetable oil rather than a cube of butter.

⊕ Buy fairly thin carrots and quarter them. They'll cook in short time. Even faster, use prepared carrot sticks from your market.

⊕ Use a wide frying pan—apples will cook faster. Also, keep pan covered to help reduce the amount of oil needed to sauté the apples.

CHILI PASTA WITH TURKEY AND LIMA BEANS

1½ cups strips of cooked turkey
¼ cup extra-virgin olive oil
1½ cups strips (about ¼ inch wide) of bottled roasted peppers
⅓ cup chopped cilantro or fresh parsley
Salt and freshly ground pepper to taste
6 ripe plum tomatoes, diced
2 cups frozen lima beans
1 pound fresh or dried chili fettuccine
Bottled hot sauce to taste (optional)

Combine turkey, 2 tablespoons oil, roasted peppers, cilantro or parsley, and salt and pepper in a large sauté pan. Cover and heat gently. Remove from heat, add tomatoes, and cover.

Cook lima beans in a large pot of boiling salted water 2 minutes. Add pasta and boil uncovered over high heat, stirring occasionally, about 3 minutes, or until pasta is tender but firm to the bite. Drain well and transfer to a large bowl. Add turkey mixture, hot sauce, and remaining 2 tablespoons oil; toss to combine. Taste and adjust seasoning.

Makes 4 servings.

CARROTS WITH CRANBERRIES AND MINT

1 pound fairly thin carrots, scraped
Pinch of salt
1 tablespoon sugar
¼ cup dried cranberries
2 teaspoons vegetable oil
½ teaspoon dried mint, crumbled

Quarter carrots lengthwise and cut into 3-inch lengths. Combine carrots, 1 cup water, and salt in a medium skillet. Cover, bring to a boil, and simmer 7 minutes over medium heat.

Add sugar, cranberries, and oil to pan. Cook uncovered over medium heat, stirring occasionally, until carrots are tender and liquid is absorbed, about 8 to 9 minutes. Watch so mixture does not burn. Stir in mint and remove from heat. Serve hot or at room temperature.

Makes 4 servings.

GRAND CANYON
APPLE CRUMBLE

1½ pounds Golden Delicious apples
1 tablespoon vegetable oil
1 teaspoon ground cinnamon
3 tablespoons sugar
4 tablespoons granola or granola-type cereal
4 scoops vanilla frozen yogurt

Peel and halve apples. Core them and cut into thin slices.

Heat oil in a large heavy nonstick skillet. Add apples and cinnamon. Cover and cook over medium-low heat, stirring often, for 8 minutes, or until apples are just tender. Add sugar. Heat just until sugar dissolves, turning apple wedges over so both sides are coated with sugar. Remove from heat.

To serve, divide warm apple mixture among 4 dessert dishes. Sprinkle each serving with 1 tablespoon granola. Top with a scoop of frozen yogurt. Serve immediately.

Makes 4 servings.

FAYE LEVY

Quick Couscous Dinner

- *Cucumber salad with yogurt and mint* •
- *Couscous with chicken and roasted peppers* •
- *Green beans with tomatoes and thyme* •
- *Apricots, peaches, or grapes* •

AMOUNT OF CALORIES FROM FAT: 17%

In Morocco, steaming mounds of couscous are often served in bowls with a tureen of broth and a platter laden with meats and vegetables. The couscous in this menu is light and luscious. It is topped with briefly braised chicken and roasted red peppers in a sauce flavored with cumin, dried onions, and chicken broth. The accompanying green beans cook rapidly, but first you need to remove the ends; try to work quickly in doing this. The light, refreshing appetizer salad can play different roles in other meals: as a topping for baked eggplant or as an accompaniment for baked potatoes, rice, or bulgur wheat.

ALTERNATIVES:

⇨ Substitute turkey breast for the chicken.
⇨ Use whole-wheat couscous, which is available in health food stores. Or if you have already cooked brown or white rice, serve the braised chicken with peppers over it, instead of using couscous.

Game Plan:

Step 1. Boil water for beans.
Step 2. Prepare beans and cook them.
Step 3. Cook chicken and couscous.
Step 4. Prepare salad.
Step 5. Finish beans with tomatoes and thyme.

Tips:

♥ The appetizer is made with nonfat yogurt and is fat-free. It's also delicious made with half yogurt and half nonfat sour cream.

☺ For a quicker side dish, substitute two 10-ounce boxes of frozen green beans for the fresh ones.

CUCUMBER SALAD WITH YOGURT AND MINT

1 small garlic clove, minced
2 teaspoons dried mint
Salt and freshly ground pepper
2 cups nonfat yogurt
1 large (European) cucumber (about 1 pound)
Small sprigs of mint (optional, for garnish)

Add garlic, mint, salt, and pepper to yogurt. Mix well.

Cut a thin slice lengthwise from one side of cucumber so cucumber holds steady. Put it on a board, cut side down. Cut cucumber into thin slices and put in a serving bowl. Add yogurt mixture and mix gently. Taste and adjust seasoning. Serve garnished with mint.

Makes 4 servings.

COUSCOUS WITH CHICKEN AND ROASTED PEPPERS

1 pound skinless, boneless chicken breast fillets
2 tablespoons olive oil
1½ teaspoons ground cumin
½ teaspoon turmeric
Salt and freshly ground pepper
1 (14½-ounce) can chicken broth
2 tablespoons dried minced onion
½ cup strips of bottled roasted red bell peppers
Harissa or other hot sauce to taste (see Note on page 114)
1 (10-ounce) package couscous (1⅔ cups)

Trim all visible fat from chicken and cut meat into 1-inch dice.

Heat oil in a large heavy sauté pan. Add chicken and sprinkle with cumin, turmeric, salt, and pepper. Sauté over medium heat for 3 minutes. Add ½ cup broth and dried onion. Stir and bring to a simmer over high heat. Cover and cook over medium-low heat about 5 minutes or until meat changes color throughout; cut a thick piece to check. Add red pepper strips and harissa to taste. Cover and keep warm.

Bring remaining broth and ¾ cup water to a boil in a small saucepan. Stir in couscous, remove from heat, and let stand 5 minutes. Taste and adjust seasoning. Serve couscous in bowls and top with chicken and its sauce.

Makes 4 servings.

GREEN BEANS WITH TOMATOES AND THYME

1½ pounds green beans, ends removed, broken into 2 pieces
2 teaspoons olive oil
1 (14½-ounce) can diced tomatoes, drained
Salt and freshly ground pepper
½ teaspoon dried thyme

Add beans to a large saucepan of boiling salted water and boil 5 to 7 minutes or until crisp-tender. Drain in a colander or strainer.

Heat oil in the same saucepan, add tomatoes, and heat over medium heat. Add beans; sprinkle with salt, pepper, and thyme and toss well. Taste and adjust seasoning. Serve hot.

Makes 4 servings.

Far Eastern Flavors

• *Carrot salad with kiwi* •

• *Sesame salmon with black fettuccine* •

• *Filipino eggplant with soy sauce and garlic* •

• *Exotic fruit and sorbet* •

AMOUNT OF CALORIES FROM FAT: 27%

Prepare this menu when you want food to be not only fast but also adventurous. For a colorful first course, try this carrot salad with fresh kiwi slices, a new light variation on the familiar grated carrot salad with raisins. The main course is a pasta and salmon salad seasoned with sesame oil vinaigrette and cilantro. Black pasta made with squid ink makes a striking presentation, but the salad is also wonderful with regular fettuccine. For dessert, try cherimoyas, guavas, blood oranges, or Asian pears. You might like to top the fruit with a scoop of passion fruit or raspberry sorbet.

ALTERNATIVES:

⇨ If you already have cooked salmon, you can use it here; for example, use the Roasted Salmon with Coriander and Lemon on page 58. Or substitute cooked lobster, crab, or shrimp; in this case, substitute canned vegetable broth for the salmon cooking liquid called for in the dressing.

⇨ For a simpler vegetable dish, instead of the eggplant, prepare steamed asparagus, spinach, or zucchini to accompany the salmon and pasta.

GAME PLAN:

Step 1. Cook salmon.
Step 2. While salmon cooks, boil water for pasta.
Step 3. Cut and cook eggplant.
Step 4. Prepare carrot salad.
Step 5. Finish salmon with pasta dish.

TIPS:

♥ Because grated carrots are sweet, you can make a dressing of twice as much vinegar as oil instead of a classic vinaigrette of three times as much oil as vinegar.

♥ By using a few spoonfuls of the flavorful salmon cooking liquid as part of the pasta dressing, you need less oil.

⊕ Buy shredded carrots at the market, or shred carrots in a food processor with a shredding disk.

CARROT SALAD WITH KIWI

1 (8-ounce) package shredded carrots (4 cups)
4 teaspoons tarragon vinegar
2 teaspoons vegetable oil
Salt and freshly ground pepper
2 kiwifruits, peeled and cut into quarter-slices

In a shallow serving bowl, mix carrots with vinegar, oil, and salt and pepper to taste. Serve topped with kiwi pieces.

Makes 4 servings.

SESAME SALMON WITH BLACK FETTUCCINE

¼ cup dry white wine
Salt
¾ pound salmon steak, about 1 inch thick
½ tablespoon vegetable oil
1 tablespoon Oriental sesame oil
½ tablespoon rice or white wine vinegar
¼ teaspoon Asian hot sauce, or more to taste
9 to 10 ounces black fettuccine or plain fettuccine or linguine
Freshly ground pepper
3 tablespoons coarsely chopped cilantro

Combine wine, 1⅓ cups water, and a pinch of salt in a small skillet. Bring to a simmer. Add salmon and return to a simmer. Cover and cook over low heat about 10 minutes, or until fish just flakes when tested with a fork. Remove salmon with a slotted spoon to a plate. Reserve liquid.

In a small bowl, whisk vegetable oil with sesame oil, vinegar, and hot sauce. Add 1½ tablespoons salmon cooking liquid.

Cook pasta in a large pot of boiling salted water 2 to 5 minutes or until just tender, al dente. Drain and transfer to a large bowl. Toss with 1 tablespoon dressing.

Meanwhile, remove skin from salmon. Pull meat into bite-size chunks, taking care to remove bones. Add salmon to bowl of pasta, add remaining dressing, and toss gently. Season to taste with salt and pepper. Add cilantro. Serve hot or cold.

Makes 4 servings.

FILIPINO EGGPLANT WITH SOY SAUCE AND GARLIC

1 large eggplant (about 1¼ pounds)
2 tablespoons vegetable oil
¼ cup distilled white vinegar
2 tablespoons soy sauce
2 large garlic cloves, minced
Freshly ground pepper
Salt (optional)
1 tablespoon chopped green onion or fresh parsley (optional)

Cut eggplant into ¾-inch dice. Heat oil in a large heavy skillet. Add eggplant cubes and sauté over medium-high heat, stirring, 2 minutes. Cover and cook over medium-low heat, stirring often, 3 minutes.

Add vinegar, soy sauce, and garlic and bring to a simmer. Cover and cook over low heat, stirring often, about 7 minutes or until eggplant is tender when pierced with a fork. Sprinkle generously with pepper; taste before adding any salt. Serve hot, sprinkled with green onion.

Makes 4 servings.

Inspiration from India

- *Fusilli with curried vegetable sauce* •
- *Easy raita (Indian tomato, cucumber, and yogurt salad* •
- *Mango and banana salad with hint of ginger* •

——————— AMOUNT OF CALORIES FROM FAT: 10% ———————

We don't associate pasta with the cuisine of India, but aromatic Indian vegetable curries are perfect with pasta and can make delectable, light menus. If you have an extra minute or two, sprinkle the finished entrée with chopped cilantro. As an accompaniment to the spicy pasta, serve cool refreshing raita. The salad's time-honored function is to calm the fire of hot curries. But it's delicious whether you're eating hot food or not, and is a terrific addition to your repertoire of quick, low-fat dishes. Raita is a great partner for cooked lentils, bulgur wheat, or brown rice and makes an appealing appetizer.

ALTERNATIVES:

⇨ In the fusilli recipe, substitute 1½ cups frozen lima beans for the chickpeas and cook them with the pasta.

⇨ Substitute 3 diced zucchini or yellow crookneck squash for the cauliflower; add them 2 to 3 minutes before pasta is done.

⇨ Serve the vegetable sauce over Basmati rice instead of mixing it with pasta.

⇨ If you don't have good mangoes, use papayas.

Game Plan:

Step 1. Heat water for pasta.
Step 2. Mince garlic in mini food processor.
Step 3. Prepare sauce for pasta; cook pasta at same time.
Step 4. Make raita.
Step 5. Make fruit salad.

Tips:

♥ With a spicy, aromatic sauce, the pasta needs only a tiny bit of oil—less than a teaspoon per portion.

☺ You can substitute prepared diced melon for the mango, but beware of peeled mango slices in jars; some brands have an unpleasant taste of preservatives.

FUSILLI WITH CURRIED VEGETABLE SAUCE

1 tablespoon vegetable oil
3 large garlic cloves, minced
1 teaspoon curry powder
½ teaspoon ground cumin
1 (14½-ounce) can diced tomatoes, drained
1 (15-ounce) can tomato sauce
½ teaspoon hot red pepper flakes, or more to taste
Salt and freshly ground pepper
1 (15-ounce can) chickpeas (garbanzo beans), drained and rinsed
8 ounces fusilli or spiral pasta (2½ cups)
3 cups small cauliflower florets

Heat oil in a heavy medium saucepan. Add garlic, curry powder, and cumin and cook over medium-low heat, stirring, ½ minute. Add tomatoes, tomato sauce, pepper flakes, salt, and pepper and stir well. Cover and bring to a boil. Uncover and cook over medium heat, stirring occasionally, 5 minutes. Add chickpeas and heat through. Taste and adjust seasoning.

Cook pasta uncovered in a large pot of boiling salted water over high heat 6 minutes. Add cauliflower and boil, stirring occasionally, 4 to 6 minutes or until pasta is tender but firm to the bite. Drain pasta mixture well and transfer to serving bowl. Toss with two-thirds of the sauce. Serve remaining sauce separately.

Makes 4 servings.

EASY RAITA (INDIAN TOMATO, CUCUMBER, AND YOGURT SALAD)

2 cups plain nonfat yogurt
½ teaspoon ground cumin
Pinch of cayenne pepper
Salt and freshly ground pepper
1 tablespoon chopped fresh mint, or 1 teaspoon dried
1 cup finely diced cucumber (¼-inch dice)
2 medium plum tomatoes, diced
Paprika, for sprinkling

Mix yogurt with cumin, cayenne, salt, and pepper. Lightly stir in mint, cucumber, and tomato. Taste and adjust seasoning. Refrigerate until ready to serve. Serve sprinkled with paprika.

Makes 4 servings.

Mango and Banana Salad with Hint of Ginger

1 large ripe mango (about ¾ pound)
2 teaspoons lime or lemon juice
2 teaspoons sugar
½ teaspoon ground ginger
2 ripe medium bananas

Cut off mango peel. Slice mango, discarding pit. Dice mango flesh and transfer to a bowl. In a cup, mix lime or lemon juice, sugar, ginger, and 1 teaspoon water. Peel and slice bananas and add to mango. Add dressing and mix gently. Serve cold.

Makes 4 servings.

Lean and Luscious Linguine Dinner

- *Tri-color vegetable salad with raspberry vinegar* •
- *Linguine with creamy mushroom sauce* •
- *Zucchini with garlic and coriander* •
- *Italian or French bread* •
- *Mixed berries or cantaloupe with vanilla frozen yogurt* •

AMOUNT OF CALORIES FROM FAT: 29%

This bright, flavorful vegetarian pasta menu is ideal for brunch or supper. The French-inspired pasta entrée has a tasty mushroom sauce that gains a creamy texture from nonfat sour cream. A savory accompaniment for the pasta is zucchini with an Egyptian seasoning blend of garlic, ground coriander, and cayenne pepper—an easy way to enhance a simply cooked vegetable. When berries are in season, try this colorful combination for dessert: 1 cup each blueberries, raspberries, and quartered strawberries served with Strawberry Sauce (page 74).

Alternatives:

⇨ If you have walnut oil, use it in the salad dressing instead of vegetable oil; it marries well with the flavor of raspberry vinegar. Or substitute balsamic vinegar for the raspberry vinegar.

⇨ Instead of the zucchini recipe, serve the pasta with boiled or steamed thin asparagus spears.

Game Plan:

Step 1. Boil pots of water for pasta and for zucchini.
Step 2. Meanwhile, prepare mushroom sauce.
Step 3. Cut zucchini, mince garlic for zucchini recipe.
Step 4. Prepare salad ingredients.
Step 5. Cook zucchini; meanwhile, cook pasta.
Step 6. Finish zucchini with garlic.
Step 7. Finish pasta.
Step 8. Dress salad.

Tips:

♥ Raspberry vinegar is a pleasant partner for greens. Its slight sweetness enables you to use less oil than in classic dressing formulas.

☺ Even if fresh linguine is kept in the freezer, it cooks in 2 or 3 minutes. There's no need to thaw it before cooking.

☺ Garlic-coriander sauce for vegetables is ready in less than a minute!

TRI-COLOR VEGETABLE SALAD WITH RASPBERRY VINEGAR

4 cups lettuce leaves, such as baby lettuce or mixed radicchio,
escarole, and endive
1 medium yellow bell pepper, cut in strips about ¼ inch wide
1 bunch arugula or basil (½ ounce)
1½ tablespoons vegetable oil
2 teaspoons raspberry vinegar
Salt and freshly ground pepper
4 medium plum tomatoes, sliced

Mix lettuce, pepper strips, and arugula or basil. Add oil, vinegar, and salt and pepper to taste. Toss well. Top with tomato slices and sprinkle them lightly with salt and pepper.

Makes 4 servings.

LINGUINE WITH CREAMY MUSHROOM SAUCE

Salt
3 tablespoons olive oil
1 pound fresh mushrooms, sliced
4 green onions, sliced
1 teaspoon dried basil
1 teaspoon dried thyme leaves
1 teaspoon paprika
Freshly ground pepper to taste
¾ cup canned chicken broth
½ cup nonfat sour cream
16 to 18 ounces fresh low-cholesterol linguine

Bring a large pot of water to a boil for cooking pasta; add salt.

Heat oil in a very large skillet. Add mushrooms, green onions, basil, thyme, paprika, salt, and pepper. Sauté over medium heat, stirring, about 3 minutes or until lightly browned. Add broth and bring to a boil over high heat. Simmer 4 minutes to thicken slightly. Remove from heat and cool 2 minutes. Stir in sour cream.

Cook linguine in boiling salted water about 2 minutes or according to package directions. Drain well. Combine with mushroom sauce in a large bowl. Toss well. Taste and adjust seasoning. Serve immediately.

Makes 4 servings.

ZUCCHINI WITH GARLIC AND CORIANDER

1¼ pounds small zucchini
1½ tablespoons olive oil
3 large garlic cloves, minced
2 teaspoons ground coriander
Salt and cayenne pepper to taste

Quarter zucchini lengthwise, then cut pieces in half crosswise. Add zucchini to a medium saucepan of boiling salted water and boil uncovered over high heat 3 minutes or until just crisp-tender. Drain well. Transfer to a shallow platter.

Heat oil in saucepan used to cook zucchini, add garlic, and cook over low heat until light brown, about 15 seconds. Add coriander and stir over low heat a few seconds to blend. Immediately add to zucchini and toss. Season to taste with salt and cayenne pepper. Serve hot.

Makes 4 servings.

Mediterranean-Style Supper

• *Spicy Moroccan carrot salad* •
• *Pasta with broccoli-garlic sauce
and sun-dried tomatoes* •
• *Melon medley with melon sorbet* •

————— AMOUNT OF CALORIES FROM FAT: 25% —————

Bold Mediterranean flavors make this menu so tempting that no-body will think it's also low in fat. It puts two healthful vegetables in the limelight: broccoli, the most popular cruciferous vegetable; and vitamin A–rich carrots. The easy appetizer will surprise anyone who thinks carrots are always matched with sweet ingredients. Here the vegetable's sweet flavor is balanced by a lemony dressing perked up with cumin and hot pepper flakes. Fresh angel-hair pasta is a fabulous choice for quick cooking, as it requires only one minute of boiling. Dessert is a quick salad of cantaloupe and honeydew melon balls with lime juice and a sprinkling of powdered sugar. It's topped with mint leaves and refreshing melon or lemon sorbet.

ALTERNATIVES:

⇨ For an appetizer of raw vegetables instead of a cooked carrot salad, serve Avocado, Red Onion, and Romaine Salad (page 108), Green Salad with Smoked Almonds and Balsamic Vinegar (page 124), or Mediterranean Chopped Salad (page 78).

⇨ In the pasta dish, instead of sun-dried tomatoes use bottled roasted red peppers.

Game Plan:

Step 1. Boil water for broccoli and pasta.
Step 2. Cook carrots for salad.
Step 3. Cook broccoli, then pasta.
Step 4. Finish carrot salad.
Step 5. Prepare melon medley.
Step 6. Finish pasta dish.

Tips:

♥ Pasta dressed with little oil should be served while still hot; if it cools, it absorbs the oil and appears dry.

♥ Sorbet is fat-free and can replace ice cream in many desserts.

① Use a pasta pot to cook broccoli, then remove it with the pot's strainer basket and use the same water to cook pasta.

SPICY MOROCCAN
CARROT SALAD

1 pound medium carrots, peeled and sliced ¼ inch thick
1½ tablespoons vegetable oil
1 medium onion, halved and sliced thin
¼ teaspoon hot red pepper flakes
½ teaspoon ground cumin
Salt and freshly ground pepper
1½ tablespoons strained fresh lemon juice

In a sauté pan, cover carrots with water, cover, and bring to a boil. Simmer over medium-high heat 5 minutes or until carrots are just tender. Remove carrots with a slotted spoon. Pour liquid into a bowl. Dry sauté pan.

Heat oil in pan from cooking carrots. Add onion and sauté over medium-high heat 2 minutes. Add ¼ cup carrot cooking liquid, pepper flakes, cumin, salt, and pepper. Bring to a boil, stirring. Reduce heat to low. Add carrots. Simmer uncovered 1 minute or until sauce coats carrots. Off heat, add lemon juice. Taste and adjust seasoning. Serve hot, warm, or cold.

Makes 4 servings.

PASTA WITH BROCCOLI-GARLIC SAUCE AND SUN-DRIED TOMATOES

2½ *quarts broccoli florets*
¼ *cup extra-virgin olive oil*
4 *large garlic cloves, chopped*
Salt and freshly ground pepper to taste
2 *(9-ounce) packages fresh angel-hair pasta*
⅔ *cup strips oil-packed sun-dried tomatoes*

Put broccoli in a pasta pot or other large pot of boiling salted water. Cover and bring to boil over high heat. Uncover and boil 3 minutes or until crisp-tender. Remove broccoli with pasta pot basket or slotted spoon, reserving water. Rinse broccoli with cold water and drain well. Chop coarsely in food processor or with knife.

Heat oil in a large heavy sauté pan over medium heat. Add garlic and sauté 5 seconds. Add broccoli, salt, and pepper and sauté about 2 minutes or until heated through.

Add pasta to the pot of boiling water. Boil uncovered over high heat 1 to 2 minutes or until tender but firm to the bite.

In a large bowl, mix pasta with broccoli sauce using tongs. Add sun-dried tomatoes; toss again. Taste and adjust seasoning. Serve hot.

Makes 4 servings.

MELON MEDLEY
WITH MELON SORBET

1 tablespoon Midori (melon liqueur) or kirsch
1 teaspoon sugar
1 teaspoon lemon or lime juice
12 cantaloupe balls
12 honeydew balls
1 pint melon, lemon, or other fruit sorbet

Mix liqueur, sugar, and lemon juice in a medium bowl. Add melon balls and toss. Cover and refrigerate until ready to serve.

To serve, spoon or scoop sorbet into 4 dessert dishes. Spoon melon balls around sorbet. Serve immediately.

Makes 4 servings.

CHAPTER 6

TEN BONUS RECIPES

SAVORY RECIPES

GRILLED MARINATED PEPPERS

Grilled bell peppers are culinary gems, adding bright color and flavor to whatever food they're paired with. You can dice the grilled peppers or cut them in strips, then mix them with cooked rice, pasta, corn, or other vegetables; or serve them with grilled chicken breasts or fish fillets. Or add these pretty peppers to salads of all types, from green salads to tuna salads.

2 medium red bell peppers
2 medium green bell peppers
2 tablespoons extra-virgin olive oil
1 to 2 teaspoons lemon juice or wine vinegar
Salt and freshly ground pepper
4 large garlic cloves, cut in quarters (optional)

Put peppers on broiler rack about 4 inches from heat. Broil peppers, turning every 4 or 5 minutes with tongs, until pepper skins are blistered and charred, 15 to 20 minutes. Transfer to a bowl and cover tightly, or put in a bag and close bag. Let stand 10 minutes. Peel using a paring knife. Discard stem, seeds, and ribs. Be careful; there may be hot liquid inside pepper. Drain well and pat dry.

Cut peppers into quarters or wide strips and put in a shallow serving dish. In a small bowl, whisk olive oil with lemon juice and salt and pepper to taste. Pour over peppers and add garlic. Let stand at room temperature, turning occasionally, 30 minutes; or refrigerate overnight. Remove garlic. Serve peppers at room temperature.

Makes 4 servings.

FAST FRESH TOMATO SALSA

Instead of dicing each ingredient by hand, make fat-free Mexican salsa cruda speedily in the food processor. This fresh salsa enlivens steamed, poached, and grilled vegetables; fish; and chicken without adding any fat. Try it over plain boiled potatoes, grilled eggplant, cauliflower, or lima beans.

2 fresh jalapeño peppers, seeds removed if desired
½ cup packed cilantro sprigs
½ medium white onion, cut in 4 pieces
¾ pound ripe plum tomatoes
Salt to taste

Wear gloves when handling hot peppers. Cut each jalapeño pepper into 4 pieces. Finely chop peppers and cilantro in a food processor. Add onion and pulse on and off until onion is chopped. Transfer mixture to a bowl. Cut green ends off tomatoes. Quarter tomatoes, add them to processor, and pulse to coarsely chop. Add to cilantro mixture and mix well. Add 2 tablespoons water. Season to taste with salt. Serve at room temperature. (Salsa can be kept 2 days in refrigerator.)

Makes about 3 cups, about 6 to 8 servings.

QUICK CILANTRO SALSA

Serve this deep green salsa with pasta, rice, corn on the cob, beans, squash, or potatoes. It's also delicious with fish and chicken. The salsa makes a great dip or dressing for raw vegetables, such as tomato and mushroom slices. It has plenty of kick, but is not excessively hot. If you would like it milder, remove the pepper seeds and ribs.

2 fresh jalapeño peppers
2 large garlic cloves, peeled
1½ cups cilantro sprigs, medium-packed
1 tablespoon extra-virgin olive oil
1 tablespoon strained fresh lime juice
3 tablespoons water
Salt to taste
¼ teaspoon ground cumin

Wear gloves when handling hot peppers. Remove seeds and ribs from peppers, if desired. Cut peppers into a few pieces. Combine peppers and garlic in a food processor and mince fine. Add cilantro and process until coarsely chopped. Transfer to a bowl and add remaining ingredients. Taste and adjust seasoning. Serve cold or at room temperature. *Salsa can be kept 2 days in refrigerator; it becomes milder as it stands.*

Makes scant ⅔ cup, about 6 servings.

YOGURT-GARLIC SAUCE

This sauce of yogurt, garlic, and fresh mint has many attributes; it's refreshing, quick, and fat-free. It is popular in Greek and Turkish cuisines for accompanying grains and vegetables. Try it with rice, bulgur wheat, lentils, or pasta, or with simply cooked vegetables such as boiled carrots, steamed zucchini, baked eggplant, or roasted peppers. The sauce is also wonderful for dressing up microwaved winter squash, potatoes, and sweet potatoes.

If your market carries extra-creamy nonfat yogurt, use it for making the sauce.

1 cup plain nonfat yogurt
1 medium garlic clove, finely minced
1 tablespoon chopped fresh mint, or ½ teaspoon dried mint
   leaves, crumbled
Salt and cayenne pepper

Mix yogurt with garlic and mint. Season to taste with salt and cayenne pepper. Serve cold or at room temperature.

Makes 1 cup, 4 servings.

FIVE-MINUTE TOMATO SAUCE

The secret to having tomato sauce thicken rapidly is to cook it in a wide pan—a skillet or sauté pan.

If you would like this sauce to be fat-free as well as fast, omit the oil and simply add the garlic to the pan along with the tomatoes. For a touch of heat, add ¼ to ½ teaspoon hot red pepper flakes with the tomatoes.

Depending on how finely you chop the tomatoes, the sauce will be quite smooth or fairly chunky. If you like it completely smooth, puree it in a food processor or blender. If you want it chunky, you can use canned diced tomatoes and then you don't need to chop them.

1 to 3 teaspoons olive oil
2 large garlic cloves, minced
2 (28-ounce) cans plum tomatoes, halved, drained, and chopped
½ teaspoon dried thyme or oregano
Salt and freshly ground pepper
2 to 3 tablespoons chopped fresh basil (optional)

Heat oil in a large deep skillet or sauté pan over medium heat. Stir in garlic. Add tomatoes, thyme, salt, and pepper. Cook uncovered over medium-high heat, stirring often, about 5 minutes or until tomatoes are soft and sauce is thick. Taste and adjust seasoning. *Sauce can be kept 2 days in refrigerator or can be frozen.* Stir in fresh basil after reheating.

Makes about 2 cups, 6 to 8 servings.

NONFAT CHEESECAKE*

It's amazing that cheesecake can taste so terrific when made with nonfat cheese. After all, traditional cheesecake is one of the richest cakes since it has only a little flour and consists mostly of cream cheese.

Crumb Crust

5 ounces graham crackers (to obtain 1¼ cups crumbs)
2 tablespoons sugar
¼ cup vegetable oil or melted margarine

Cheese Filling

1 (15-ounce) container fat-free ricotta cheese (1¾ cups)
¾ cup nonfat sour cream
¾ cup sugar
2 large eggs, separated
2 tablespoons all-purpose flour
Grated rind of 1 large lemon (1½ teaspoons)
1 teaspoon vanilla extract

Yogurt Topping

½ cup plain nonfat yogurt
1 cup nonfat sour cream
3 tablespoons sugar
1 teaspoon vanilla extract

*Strictly speaking, there is a small amount of fat in the crust and the eggs, but the cake contains no butterfat because of the fat-free cheeses.

To make the crust: Preheat oven to 350°F. Process crackers in a food processor to fine crumbs, or put them in a bag and crush them with a rolling pin. Measure 1¼ cups. Mix crumbs with sugar in a bowl. Add oil and mix well. Lightly grease a 9-inch springform pan. Press crumb mixture in an even layer on bottom and about 1 inch up sides of pan. Bake 8 minutes. Let cool completely. Leave oven at 350°F.

To make the cheese filling: Beat ricotta cheese with sour cream at low speed until very smooth. Gradually beat in sugar. Beat in egg yolks, flour, lemon rind, and vanilla. In a small bowl, whip egg whites until stiff. Fold them into cheese mixture. Carefully pour filling into cooled crust. Bake about 50 minutes or until top center is just firm but still shakes when you gently move the pan; cracks will form in cake. Remove from oven and cool 15 minutes. Raise oven temperature to 425°F.

To make the topping: Pour off any water from top of yogurt. Mix yogurt with sour cream, sugar, and vanilla. Spoon topping evenly over cake in spoonfuls. Carefully spread topping in an even layer, without letting it drip over edge of cake. Return cake to oven and bake 7 minutes. Cool to room temperature. Refrigerate at least 2 hours before serving. *Cake can be kept 3 days in refrigerator.* Remove sides of springform pan a short time before serving.

Makes 8 to 10 servings.

FAST FAT-FREE
RICE PUDDING

When I was researching the desserts of France, I found that rice pudding is loved throughout that country, from Provence to Normandy. Home cooks use a time-honored technique of baking the rice with milk and butter for three hours.

Rice pudding is a favorite in America, too. In my home it has always been the ultimate comfort food. I decided to devise a quick, low-fat way to prepare the dessert so that my family could enjoy it often.

First I took advantage of a tip I learned in Paris from a professional chef. He boiled the rice for three minutes in water before cooking it in milk, thus shortening its cooking time considerably. I took this idea further by blanching the rice in water a few minutes longer until it was half cooked, and then simmered it in milk. The total cooking time was under twenty-five minutes.

The next challenge was to prepare a delicious rice pudding without any fat. To achieve a creamy consistency, I opted for Arborio rice, the type used for risotto. Even when I used nonfat milk and no butter, this variety of rice still produced a luscious rice pudding.

To flavor rice puddings, I add a vanilla bean or a cinnamon stick to the simmering milk, or I stir vanilla extract or grated orange or lemon rind into the cooked pudding. When I lived in France, I used to add candied fruit, but now I prefer dried fruit—golden or dark raisins, or dried cherries, blueberries, or cranberries. Adding the fruit to the still-hot rice mixture makes it plump and tender.

Rice pudding is a convenient dessert to make because most of us have the ingredients on hand. Use a heavy saucepan and stir the rice often as it cooks in the milk, to prevent it from scorching. Choose a large saucepan so the milk will not boil over.

¾ cup white rice, preferably Arborio or other short-grained rice
3 cups nonfat milk
Pinch of salt
4½ tablespoons sugar
¼ cup raisins or dried cherries
1½ teaspoons vanilla extract
Cinnamon for sprinkling (optional)

Bring 6 cups water to a boil in a large heavy saucepan and add rice. Boil uncovered 7 minutes; drain well.

Bring milk to a boil in same saucepan over medium-high heat, stirring occasionally. Add rice and salt. Cook uncovered over medium-low heat, stirring often, about 15 minutes or until rice is very soft and absorbs most of milk. Rice should look creamy, not soupy and not dry. Stir in sugar. Cook 1 minute, stirring. Remove from heat and stir in raisins and vanilla. Serve warm, sprinkled with cinnamon.

Makes 4 servings.

CHOCOLATE PECAN BROWNIES

Substituting fruit purees for fat has become a popular baking principle in the past few years. I have applied this technique in these brownies by using apple butter to reduce the fat to less than half the customary amount in brownies. Instead of butter, this recipe has a small amount of vegetable oil. I have reduced the amount of chocolate and reinforced the chocolate taste by adding cocoa, which is low in fat. The result is flavorful cakelike brownies with a pleasant texture. When you eat them, you don't know they are low-fat.

To save time, buy pecan pieces instead of dicing pecan halves; they often cost less, too.

2 ounces semisweet chocolate, chopped
¼ cup vegetable oil
⅓ cup apple butter (available in jars)
⅓ cup unsweetened cocoa
¾ cup all-purpose flour
½ teaspoon baking soda
¼ teaspoon salt
2 large eggs
½ cup packed brown sugar
½ cup granulated sugar
½ cup diced pecans

Position rack in center of oven and preheat to 350°F. Line base and sides of an 8-inch square baking pan with a single piece of waxed paper or foil; lightly oil paper or foil.

Melt chocolate in a medium bowl over nearly simmering water. Stir until smooth. Remove from pan of water. Stir in oil and apple butter. Sift cocoa, flour, baking soda, and salt into a small bowl.

Beat eggs lightly in large bowl. Add sugars; beat until blended. Whip mixture at high speed about 5 minutes or until thick and light. Gradually stir in melted chocolate mixture at low speed just until blended. Stir in cocoa mixture, then pecans; do not overmix.

Pour batter into prepared pan. Bake about 30 minutes or until a wooden pick inserted into center of mixture comes out nearly clean. Cool in pan on a rack to room temperature. Turn out onto a tray; remove paper or foil. Cut in 2-inch squares to serve.

Makes 16 brownies.

MANGO SAUCE

I love this flavorful sauce with lemon or kiwi sorbet, vanilla frozen yogurt, or fruit salad. Some markets carry frozen peeled diced mango or frozen mango puree, which are the fastest, easiest choices for making the sauce; use about 1¼ cups diced mango or about 1 cup frozen puree. I do not recommend using the peeled mango slices available in jars.

1½ to 1¾ pounds ripe mango
5 to 6 tablespoons confectioners' sugar, sifted
1 to 2 teaspoons fresh lemon or lime juice (optional)
1 to 2 teaspoons rum (optional)

Peel mango using a paring knife. Cut flesh from pit. Puree fruit in food processor or blender. Add 5 tablespoons confectioners' sugar. Process until very smooth. Strain into a bowl, pressing on pulp in strainer. Use a rubber spatula to scrape mixture from underside of strainer.

Taste sauce and whisk in more sugar if needed. Whisk to blend well. If lumps of sugar remain, strain sauce again. Cover and refrigerate 30 minutes. *Sauce can be kept, covered, 1 day in refrigerator.* Stir before serving and add lemon juice or rum if desired. Serve cold.

Makes about 1 cup, 4 servings.

Raspberry Sauce

This brilliant-colored, fresh-tasting sauce is also known as Melba sauce, as it's used to prepare the classic dessert peach Melba, with peaches and vanilla ice cream. You can make a low-fat version of that dessert by combining this sauce with peaches and vanilla frozen yogurt or ice milk. Or simply serve the frozen yogurt topped with raspberry sauce and garnished with a mixture of berries.

If you keep raspberries in your freezer, you always have the ingredients to make this sauce to dress up a great variety of desserts. Serve it with angel food cake, Nonfat Cheesecake (page 173), or other low-fat cakes. Raspberry sauce is also fabulous mixed with diced fresh soft fruit, such as nectarines, peaches, ripe pears, berries, melon balls, and orange segments, for a luscious fruit salad.

3 cups (about 12 ounces) fresh raspberries, or 1 (10- to 12-ounce) package frozen unsweetened or lightly sweetened raspberries, thawed
⅔ cup confectioners' sugar, sifted
1 to 2 teaspoons framboise (clear raspberry brandy) or kirsch or 1 tablespoon raspberry liqueur (optional)
1 to 2 teaspoons fresh lemon or lime juice (optional)

Puree berries in food processor or blender. Add confectioners' sugar. Process until very smooth. Strain into a bowl, pressing on pulp in strainer; use rubber spatula to scrape mixture from underside of strainer.

Taste sauce and whisk in more sugar if needed. Whisk to blend well. Cover and refrigerate 30 minutes. *Sauce can be kept, covered, 1 day in refrigerator.* Stir before serving and add spirits or lemon juice if desired. Serve cold.

Makes about 1 cup, 4 servings.

CONVERSION CHART

LIQUID MEASURES

Fluid Ounces	U.S. Measures	Imperial Measures	Milliliters
	1 tsp.	1 tsp.	5
1/4	2 tsp.	1 dessert spoon	7
1/2	1 T.	1 T.	15
1	2 T.	2 T.	28
2	1/4 cup	4 T.	56
4	1/2 cup or 1/4 pint		110
5		1/4 pint or 1 gill	140
6	3/4 cup		170
8	1 cup or 1/2 pint		225
9			250 (1/4 liter)
10	1-1/4 cups	1/2 pint	280
12	1-1/2 cups or 3/4 pint		340
15		3/4 pint	420
16	2 cups or 1 pint		450
18	2-1/4 cups		500 (1/2 liter)
20	2-1/2 cups	1 pint	560
24	3 cups or 1-1/2 pints		675
25		1-1/4 pints	700
27	3-1/2 cups		750
30	3-3/4 cups	1-1/2 pints	840
32	4 cups or 2 pints or 1 quart		900
35		1-3/4 pints	980
36	4-1/2 cups		1000 (1 liter)

SOLID MEASURES

U.S. and Imperial Measures		Metric Measures	
Ounces	Pounds	Grams	Kilos
1		28	
2		56	
3-1/2		100	
4	1/4	112	
5		140	
6		168	
8	1/2	225	
9		250	1/4
12	3/4	340	
16	1	450	
18		500	1/2
20	1-1/4	560	
24	1-1/2	675	
27		750	3/4
28	1-3/4	780	
32	2	900	
36	2-1/4	1000	1
40		1100	
48	3	1350	
54		1500	1-1/2

OVEN TEMPERATURE EQUIVALENTS

Fahrenheit	Gas Mark	Celsius	Heat of Oven
225	1/4	107	Very Cool
250	1/2	121	Very Cool
275	1	135	Cool
300	2	148	Cool
325	3	163	Moderate
350	4	177	Moderate
375	5	190	Fairly Hot
400	6	204	Fairly Hot
425	7	218	Hot
450	8	232	Very Hot
475	9	246	Very Hot

INDEX

F

Fall Favorites with a New Twist, 137–140
Far Eastern Flavors, 146–150
Fast Fat-Free Rice Pudding, 175–176
  in New Year's menu, 101
Fast Fresh Tomato Salsa, 169
  in Mexican vegetarian menu, 106
Fat-Free Fusilli with Peas and Tomatoes, 133
  in Provençal fish menu, 65
Filet Mignon Feast for Two, 13–17
Filipino Eggplant with Soy Sauce and Garlic, 150
Fish and seafood
  broiled, 5–6
  in California menu, 70–74
  choosing, 1–2
  cioppino, 73
  cod, barbecued on lettuce, 35
  cod, barbecued, as substitute for crab, 75
  cooking tip, 66
  crab with couscous, mint, and toasted pine nuts, 77
  crab, as substitute for salmon, 146
  Hawaiian escolar, as substitute for salmon, 56
  lobster, as substitute for crab, 75
  lobster, as substitute for salmon, 146
  menus, 55–89
  microwaving, 8
  poaching, 7
  Provençal menu, 65–69
  in salads, 10, 38
  salmon with black fettuccine, 149
  salmon dinner menu, 55–59
  salmon, roasted with coriander and lemon, 58
  salmon, as substitute for crab, 75
  scallops, as substitute for shrimp, 80, 85
  sea bass, broiled with garlic and rosemary, 67
  sea bass, as substitute for salmon, 56
  sea bass, as substitute for scallops, 71
  sea bass, as substitute for sole, 60
  shrimp, as substitute for crab, 75
  shrimp, as substitute for salmon, 146
  shrimp dinner menu, 80–84
  shrimp fiesta menu, 85–89
  shrimp in red pepper saffron sauce, 88
  shrimp in spicy tomato sauce, 83
  shrimp salad, 40
  smoked, as substitute for crab, 75
  sole menu, 60–64
  sole, sautéed with mushrooms, lettuce, and warm vinaigrette, 63
  tuna, as substitute for crab, 75
Five-Minute Tomato Sauce, 172
Frozen Yogurt with Dark Chocolate Sauce, 130
Fruit
  choosing, 2–3
  in green salads, 10
  with honey-yogurt sauce, 135
  mango sauce, 179
  melon, with melon sorbet, 165
  nectarines in red wine, 69
  papayas as substitute for mangos, 151
  pear and kiwi salad, 37
  pineapple with melon balls and rum syrup, 53
  raspberry sauce, 180
  salad, mango and banana, 155
  salad, pear and strawberry, 125
  salad, preparation tips, 34
  salad, summer berry with framboise, 79
  snacking, 12
  strawberries, chocolate dipped, 64
  See also Desserts
Fusilli with Curried Vegetable Sauce, 153

G

Garlic
   artichokes and rice with, 89
   beef salad with pasta, tomatoes,
      and, 123
   broccoli sauce, 164
   chicken soup with broccoli and, 36
   chili potatoes with, 84
   eggplant with soy sauce and, 150
   sea bass broiled with rosemary
      and, 67
   sirloin steak barbecued with, 20
   spinach, 104
   yogurt sauce, 171
   zucchini and coriander with, 160
Garlic-Scented Spinach, 104
Ginger-Scented Broccoli, 59
Grand Canyon Apple Crumble, 140
   in salmon dinner menu, 56
   in spaghetti dinner menu, 127
Greek Salad with Feta Cheese, 98
Greek Vegetarian Dinner, 96–100
Green beans
   boiling method, 7
   in minestrone, 117
Green Beans with Tomatoes and
   Thyme, 145
Green salad
   with artichoke hearts and
      chickpeas, 128
   with mushrooms and walnut oil,
      94
   with Vidalia onions, 18
Green Salad with Smoked Almonds
   and Balsamic Vinegar, 124
   in California seafood menu, 71
   in Mediterranean supper menu,
      161
Grilled Lamb Chops with Cumin, 30
Grilled Marinated Peppers, 167–168
Grilling, 5–6

H

Hawaiian escolar, as substitute for
   salmon, 56
Honey-Yogurt Sauce, 135
   in North African menu, 111

I

Indian-inspired dishes, 151–155
Indian Tomato, Cucumber, and
   Yogurt Salad, 154
Italian Salad with Artichoke Hearts,
   128

J

Jicama and Red Pepper Salad, 82

K

Kiwi
   carrot salad with, 148
   pear salad with dried cranberries,
      37

L

Lamb
   chops, grilled with cumin, 30
   dinner menu, 28–32
   in spaghetti sauce, 127
Lean and Luscious Linguine Dinner,
   156–160
Leftovers, 11
Light Pesto, 119
Lima beans
   chili pasta with turkey and, 138
   as substitute for black-eyed peas,
      101
   as substitute for chickpeas, 151
Linguine with Creamy Mushroom
   Sauce, 159

S

Saffron sauce, red pepper, 88
Sage-tomato sauce, 25
Saint Tropez Tomato Salad, 68
  in southern-style steak menu, 18
Salad of Baby Lettuces, 27
  in filet mignon menu, 13
  in lamb dinner menu, 28
Salads
  avocado, red onion, and romaine,
    108
  baby lettuce, 27
  barbecued cod on lettuce, 35
  broccoli slaw, 18
  carrot, spicy, 163
  carrot with kiwi, 148
  coleslaw, 19
  coleslaw with mustard dressing, 22
  corn, with sun-dried tomatoes and
    dill dressing, 93
  cucumber, with yogurt and mint,
    143
  dinner, 57
  dressings, 10
  fruit. *See under* Fruit
  Greek, with feta cheese, 98
  green, with artichoke hearts and
    chickpeas, 128
  green, with mushrooms and
    walnut oil, 94
  green, with smoked almonds and
    balsamic vinegar, 124
  green, with Vidalia onions, 18
  Indian tomato, cucumber, and
    yogurt, 154
  Italian, with artichoke hearts and
    chickpeas, 128
  jicama and red pepper, 82
  Mediterranean, 65
  Mediterranean chopped, 78
  and menu planning, 9–10
  pasta and roast beef, with garlic
    and tomatoes, 123
  red cabbage, with tarragon
    dressing, 134
  red cabbage, with walnuts and
    orange, 105
  shrimp, with greens, 40
  sliced vegetable, with capers, 87
  soup and, supper menu, 91–96
  spinach, with bell peppers and
    herb dressing, 72
  spinach, with orange and red
    onion, 113
  summer feast menu, 75–79
  tips for making, 24
  tomato, 68
  vegetable, with raspberry vinegar,
    158
  See also Vegetables
Salmon
  cooking tips, 55, 56
  dinner menu, 55–59
  roasted with coriander and lemon,
    58
  as substitute for crab, 75
  substitutes for, 56, 146
Salsa
  cilantro, 170
  tomato, 169
Sauces
  broccoli-garlic, 164
  mushroom meat, 129
  red pepper saffron, 88
  thickening method, 86
  tomato, 172
  tomato-sage, 25
  yogurt-garlic, 171
Sauces, dessert
  dark chocolate, 130
  honey-yogurt, 135
  mango, 179
  raspberry, 180
  strawberry, 74
Sautéed Sole with Mushrooms,
    Lettuce, and Warm Vinaigrette,
    63
Sautéing, 6
Scallops
  cioppino, with shrimp, 73
  cooking tip, 71
  substitute for, 71
  as substitute for shrimp, 80, 85
Sea bass
  broiled with garlic and rosemary,
    67
  as substitute for salmon, 56

as substitute for scallops, 71
as substitute for sole, 60
Seafood. *See* Fish and seafood; *specific kinds*
Seasoning
  broiled foods, 5
  vegetables, 7
Sesame Salmon with Black Fettuccine, 149
Shellfish. *See* Fish and seafood; *specific kinds*
Shopping, 1–4
Shrimp
  cioppino, with scallops, 73
  dinner menu, 80–84
  in red pepper saffron sauce, 88
  salad, with greens, 40
  for salads, 10
  in Spanish fiesta menu, 85–89
  in spicy tomato sauce, 83
  as substitute for crab, 75
  as substitute for salmon, 146
  substitutes for, 80, 85
Sliced Vegetable Salad with Capers, 87
  in Provençal fish menu, 65
Snacking, 12
Soft-Serve Strawberry Sorbet with Fresh Fruit, 74
Sorbet
  melon, 165
  strawberry, 74
Soup
  chicken-noodle with broccoli and garlic, 36
  minestrone, 118
  onion and winter squash, 95
  and salad, in supper menu, 91–96
Southern-Style Steak Menu, 18–21
South-of-the-Border Vegetarian Meal, 106–110
Spaghetti with Mushroom Meat Sauce, 129
Spanish Shrimp Fiesta, 85–89
Speedy Sweet-and-Sour Chicken, 41
Spicy Black Beans, 109
Spicy Moroccan Carrot Salad, 163
Spicy Shrimp Dinner, Southwest Style, 80–84

Spinach
  garlic-scented, 104
  steaming method, 8
Spinach Salad with Bell Peppers and Herb Dressing, 72
  in salmon dinner menu, 56
  in soup and salad supper menu, 92
Spinach Salad with Orange and Red Onion, 113
  in soup and salad supper menu, 92
Springtime Lamb Dinner with Middle Eastern Flavors, 28
Springtime Sole menu, 60–64
Squash
  microwaving, 8
  in minestrone, 117
  as substitute for cauliflower, 151
  winter, soup, 95
  yellow, in brown rice with tomatoes, 110
Steak. *See* Beef
Steamed Rice, 42
  in shrimp fiesta menu, 85
Steamed Zucchini with Hot Cilantro Dressing, 48
Steaming, 8
Stir-frying, 6
Stir-Fry of Peppers and Green Onion, 43
Strawberries
  chocolate-dipped, 64
  crepes, 17
  salad, with pears, 125
  sorbet, with fresh fruit, 74
Strawberry Sauce, 74
Sugar Snap Peas with Shallots, 16
Summer Berry Salad with Framboise, 79
  in sole menu, 60
Summer Brunch with Italian Flavors, 121–125
Summer Salad Feast, 75–79
Sun-dried tomatoes
  in broccoli-garlic pasta sauce, 164
  buying tip, 92
  in corn salad, 93
Sweet-and-sour chicken, 41
Swiss chard, in minestrone, 117

T

V

spinach, garlic-scented, 104
spinach, in minestrone, 117
squash, in minestrone, 117
squash, as substitute for
cauliflower, 151
steaming, 8
sugar snap peas with shallots, 16
swiss chard, in minestrone, 117
tomatoes, in minestrone, 118
tomatoes, pasta with peas and, 133
tomatoes and yellow squash in
brown rice, 110
zucchini, in minestrone, 118
zucchini, steamed with hot cilantro
dressing, 48
zucchini, as substitute for
cauliflower, 151
zucchini with garlic coriander, 160
zucchini with orzo and saffron, 26
See also Beans; Peas; Salads; *specific
kinds*
Vegetarian menus, 91–122
Vinegar
balsamic, 124
raspberry, 157, 158
rice, 39
tarragon, 134
types, 10

W

Walnut oil, 92, 94, 157
Winter squash. *See* Squash

Y

Yogurt
cucumber salad with mint and, 143
sauce with honey, 135
Yogurt-Garlic Sauce, 171

Z

Zucchini
boiling method, 7
in minestrone, 118
with orzo and saffron, 26
sautéing, 6
steamed, with hot cilantro
dressing, 48
steaming method, 8
as substitute for cauliflower, 151
Zucchini with Garlic and Coriander,
160

ABOUT THE AUTHOR

Award-winning author Faye Levy has lived and cooked on three continents—Europe, Asia, and North America—and has written fifteen cookbooks in three languages. Her most recent book award was bestowed on her latest book, *Faye Levy's International Vegetable Cookbook*, which won a James Beard Cookbook Award. This book was the third volume in her "International" series for Warner Books.

For the past five years Faye has been a nationally syndicated cooking columnist for the *Los Angeles Times* Syndicate, with a biweekly column called "Quick and Classy." In her column she emphasizes fast, easy, delicious dishes that are low in fat.

Faye has written many feature articles for *Gourmet* and *Bon Appétit* magazines. For six years she was a monthly columnist of *Bon Appétit*, writing "The Basics" column. Her articles have also appeared in *Cook's*, *Simply Seafood*, and *Western Chef* magazines.

Faye holds the "Grand Diplôme" of the first graduating class of the famous Parisian cooking school La Varenne, where she spent nearly six years working closely with the school's chefs. She is especially pleased that she coauthored a cookbook in France, *La Cuisine du Poisson*, with her favorite teacher, Master Chef Fernand Chambrette.

Faye teaches cooking and food writing at Santa Monica College, UCLA, and cooking schools in California. She and her husband/associate Yakir Levy live in Woodland Hills, California.